Enjoying Retirement

Enjoying Retirement

LIVING LIFE TO THE FULLEST

Leonard Doohan

Paulist Press
New York/Mahwah, NJ

Cover and book design by Sharyn Banks

Library of Congress Cataloging-in-Publication Data

Doohan, Leonard.
    Enjoying retirement : living life to the fullest / Leonard Doohan.
      p. cm.
    Includes bibliographical references.
    ISBN 978-0-8091-4635-2 (alk. paper)
    1. Retirees—Religious life. 2. Retirement—Religious aspects—Christianity.
I. Title.
    BV4596.R47D66 2010
    248.8´5—dc22

                                   2009046453

Published by Paulist Press
997 Macarthur Boulevard
Mahwah, New Jersey 07430

www.paulistpress.com

Printed and bound in the
United States of America

Contents

I dedicate this book to Dr. Marlene Moore
and Dr. Zia Yamayee—
colleagues for a while,
friends for over twenty years,
family by choice—
with love and gratitude.

Acknowledgments

I would like to thank the many retirees from all walks of life who completed questionnaires for me and participated in interviews, some of whom sent detailed reflections on their retirement. Their thoughts are found throughout the book. I was fortunate to receive their input and was moved by their enthusiasm and joy in retirement and by their wisdom in carefully planning and prioritizing this special time.

I also thank Fr. Michael Kerrigan, editor at Paulist Press, for his constant care in guiding the manuscript to completion. I feel fortunate to have Fr. Kerrigan as editor for the second time and to benefit from his skills. He always improves the work.

I thank my wife, Helen, with whom I share my retirement years. She has done and continues to do so much to enrich our own retirement and thereby has also contributed to this book.

Preface

(Taken from a personal journal)

Friday, January 18, 2002

Today I retired after twenty-seven years with the same organization and after forty-two years of working life. At 2:30 in the afternoon I left the building where my office has been for the past twelve years, said good-bye to my staff, and quietly walked away. I was calm and peaceful. Fortunately, I didn't meet anyone on the way out since I doubt my facade of calmness would have held up. I have given my life to this organization for the last twenty-seven years, and it too has given me life—not just opportunity for employment, salary, and the ever-important pension, but the chance to do what I wanted to do with my life, and to be the kind of person I wanted to be. I am grateful for the times I have spent there, and I am sure the loss I feel will at times grow and at times fade into the background in the months and years ahead. I feel funny; I don't know whether to be upset or to celebrate. It's a risk to make this decision but it would have been a risk not to have made it. I am just sixty and I could have worked for several more years. I had a good salary; in fact, in these last two years I have had a great salary, and I have chosen to leave at the very time when I am beginning to earn more than I ever thought I would.

I can't believe I am retired. How on earth did I arrive at this decision? Is the timing right? I don't think I have ever identified myself with my job or with my title, but I have neither now. It must be terrible for those people whose self-identity was based on their position and work. Still I do find the word *retire* rather oppressive. I certainly don't think I am retiring if that means withdrawing from the day's work into a period of rest. I feel I am on the threshold of a new period in life, perhaps the most important period in life today, and I would like to hope I can make the most of it. But for now I need to be at peace, grateful for the past and for those who have made it possible, and open to a new future that is not clear, but neither is it threatening. I think being retired might be okay after all.

Looking Forward to a New Beginning

Retirement as a New Beginning

"Christian life is a movement from beginnings to beginnings through beginnings that never end" (Gregory of Nyssa, early Christian writer). This is true every day of our lives, as we rise from failure to rededicate ourselves to the Lord Jesus. However, it is particularly true for each of us as we move through the important stages of our lives, striving to be faithful to the Lord as circumstances change. Perhaps no stage in life is more important in calling us to begin anew than the transition to retirement. Making our lives meaningful from the perspective of faithful dedication to the Lord takes on special significance when the period in question is our last.

Retirement is a time for a new beginning, a time to face change and transition with a renewal of commitment to those values felt deep in our hearts. Retirement is an opportunity to appreciate the gift of time like never before and to use our time well. It is a period of grace to be who we want to be and to do what we want to do with our lives. Retirement can be a generous time for

1

each of us, as we share with others the wisdom and experiences of our own lives with their many ups and downs. Retirement is an opportunity to clarify once and for all our purposes and destinies in life, and a time to get the best out of each moment, pursuing with a passion the call the Lord has placed in each of us. As we move toward and through retirement, it becomes clearer that our future will inevitably include physical decline and death, and that we are called to approach these, too, with the dignity of our Christian calling.

Religions have often considered the last period of a person's life as a time of withdrawal. As one's duties in life came to a conclusion, a person could withdraw from the cares of the world and concentrate on the things that matter. However, the Second Vatican Council defined the autonomy of earthly realities, specifying that worldly values are good, and that Christians should use them well to the glory of God. The bishops in the council even proclaimed that the good things of this world are not only to be used well; they should be enjoyed as gifts of God. So, nowadays we no longer prove the Christian values of our lives by withdrawing from our modern world and its developments, as retirees did in former times, but rather we maintain our Christian values amid all the changes that retirement brings. Hence, Christians should enjoy this period of their lives, as they also yearn to give focus to their faith values.

This book is on the spirituality of retirement, offering both practical advice to retirees while challenging them to approach this period of life with fidelity to the inner values of their hearts. This book is for a new kind of retiree—including the baby-boomer generation—who seeks to deal with retirement years not as an end of usefulness but as a major period in life with its own challenges that need practical responses and depth of understanding. Christian spirituality refers to the way we live our daily lives in the challenge of faith. Clearly, the years of retirement offer the most important occasion for each of us to respond to this challenge of making a new beginning.

Retirement and Faith

Retirement is a time to draw together the motivating values of our faith and to construct once and for all an adult personality in faith. Throughout our lives, we may have striven to dedicate ourselves to the Lord, but as human conditions and circumstances change, we need to adapt and live our commitment in new situations. Therefore, spirituality is not some emotional feeling of devotion; it is a commitment in love through faith and hope that leads to a greater enrichment of life. It takes as its starting point the life we live in the world we know. For retirees the new beginning is the transition into a period after active employment or engagement with family. The key components of the retiree's new life are facing transition, living prudently, using free time well, being creative in changed situations, sharing experiences, prioritizing values, focusing on growth of the inner self, accepting decline, and dying with dignity. Each of these components is a chapter in this book. These are the components that become the foundation of retirees' spiritual renewal, as they are also components for a joy-filled retirement.

There are three dimensions to living faith. First, our expressions of faith must be rooted in the experience that gave birth to faith. For Christians this is Jesus' life and teachings, as they are the motivation for all we do and all we want to be. We constantly look at our lives alongside those initial Christian experiences to make sure we are faithful to the sources of our lives. However, that experience of Jesus took place over 2,000 years ago, and written explanations of those events as we find in the Bible tell us what discipleship was like 2,000 years ago.

Therefore, the second dimension of our faith is that we need to interpret those past events so that they have relevance in today's changed circumstances of history and culture. We need to make what was spirit and life 2,000 years ago spirit and life for us today. *Not* to interpret these insights into relevant contemporary expressions would mean letting something that was life-giving in the past fossilize for today's believers.

The third dimension of faith arises at times when circumstances are very different from what they have been. We need courageous people to explore new ways of living out the faith-filled message in circumstances never encountered before. This third dimension gives rise to new spiritualities for the ages. These three dimensions—

rootedness, interpretation, and discovery—are what keep faith living and life-giving. Since today's new retirees are different from their predecessors, they must find new ways of being faithful to perennial values.

Retirement is a time of grace, when individuals can refocus their lives on the values of faith. Faith is concretely expressed in making decisions about important issues. We have already seen the key areas of retirees' lives—those which form the basis of each of the chapters of this book. These are the areas of life in which retirees manifest their faith and values. They will need to keep an eye on the foundational events of Jesus' experience, interpret them for today, and finally explore and discover new ways of living out Christian spirituality in the changed circumstances of their newfound contemporary lives.

Retirement as a New Outlook on Life

As we move from beginnings to beginnings through beginnings that never end, Jesus constantly reminds us of his challenge to conversion—to a change of heart. Heart in Jesus' time was thought to be the source of knowledge not love, and Jesus' words can be translated as "get a new outlook on life." This is the vocation of contemporary retirees. The new outlook that retirees need to have will include the following components:

1. Live in peace and not with the worries of former times. Retirement can be a wonderful transition to the best of times and an opportunity for retirees to present society with a new understanding of retirement. This movement to fullness of life can be done in peace, without emphasizing the worries of former periods in life. Retirees can move to this new phase in life with optimism and joy.

2. Focus on new attitudes beyond those of the employment years. Retirement is a time of major changes in employment, health, home, and relationships. Change becomes an integral part of life, and we focus our attention on new priorities and values. We will need to let go of competitive approaches from our working life and focus instead on peace, hope, enthusiasm, and optimism. It is also a time to give a renewed importance to family, friends, and well-chosen advisors.

3. Look at the enriching opportunities of relaxation and leisure. One of the most notable features of retirement is free time. Having control over one's time is one of the most welcoming features of retirement according to many retirees. Time is open-ended and in abundance, a luxury rarely experienced by most of us during our employment years. The question is how to approach the use of time. Genuine leisure is not the inevitable result of free time. Fostering a Christian approach to the use of time and becoming witnesses to a healthy balanced life are key responsibilities of one's retirement years.

4. Keep an eye on creative self-development. Retirees have the time to think differently, to act differently, and to be different, and many of them choose to use the opportunities offered. Retirees not only have time but also the opportunity to carefully discern and to critically assess alternatives, and to focus on what they choose. These gifts of time, of clarity, and of focus lead to opportunities for synthesis, the ability to see things in relation to each other, to see connections and interrelationships that can bring insight and creative assessment. All these qualities come together to bring peace and to make retirement years a great opportunity for creative involvement.

5. *Look at life as an opportunity to share wisdom and experience with others.* The inward journey to our deepest-held values is a journey one can make in retirement. It brings to light the values and failures of one's life. This careful scrutiny is part of the slow process that retirees can use to bring perspective, insight, and wisdom to others in volunteer work, in healing divisions, in dealing with others' pain, and in making peace. Retirement is a time when one can return to essential values that have guided and still guide choices in life. This is a journey that helps one to live a value-centered existence, and to judge everything by the measure of love. This is an awesome and exciting challenge for retirees.

6. *Get the best out of life, not more.* Retirees learn to establish a new attitude to time, a new pace of living, and a new sense of routine. Retirees need a new sense of purpose in doing what is worthwhile and pursuing it with a passion. This means deliberately removing boredom and building an exciting life that brings happiness.

As retirees, we need to do this with awareness of our age; it means stressing preventive care, focusing on positive attitudes, and planning for the future. Above all, reflection should permeate all that we do.

7. *Follow the direction of the Spirit.* There is nothing more important for retirees than spirituality—that focus on their fidelity to the inner values of their hearts. These values come from peak experiences in their lives and motivate them to become the best they are capable of being. Spirituality for retirees will embrace, affect, and color every aspect of life. It is that constant call to be more authentic in how we live and respond to others and to our world.

8. *Maintain wellness, and let the quality of life determine the quality of death.* It is impossible to deal with retirement outside a consideration of the aging process. We must all deal with the experience of aging, manage the various additional stresses that we encounter as we age, and learn how to live gracefully with the chronic conditions of later life experiences. Our challenge is to strive for wellness at each stage of life, living the best we are capable of at each moment. One of the characteristics of people as they get older is they think more and more about final realities—end-of-life issues, the reality of death, whether there is an afterlife, what it would be like, is there a God, and so on. How one chooses to live in this world is ultimately determined by what one thinks will happen at the end of life. For Christians, dying with dignity is the natural sequel to living with faith.

A WONDERFUL OPPORTUNITY

Retirement can be a wonderful opportunity for a full life that is permeated with Christian values. This book emphasizes the key areas of contemporary retirees' lives. Throughout each chapter I present the comments of retirees I have interviewed or who have responded to questionnaires I have distributed. Their ideas punctuate the text, and their advice is in every chapter. Their excitement and anxieties as they approach this new period of life immerse the reader in the experience of retirement.

Retirement has its own spirituality. It challenges each of us to approach this stage in life with enthusiasm and anticipation, developing this stage in life—as much as a third of life for many—for its own sake as the best period in our lives and as a time to enhance our lives with values that mean the most to us.

1 *Discovering New Opportunities*

FOCUS POINTS OF THIS CHAPTER:

- Entrusting fears and hopes for retirement to the Lord

- Letting spiritual values become an integral part of this new transition

- Finding joy in retirement years by making a difference in other people's lives

- Approaching this period of life with a new discovery of Christian values

What a Transition! The Voices of Retirees

When I asked a large group of retirees how they would describe their present life, the responses were interesting. *"These are the best of times!" "Life has been good to me." "Contentment." "Right now—great!" "I am joyful and grateful." "Casual."*

A retired real estate manager said, *"Life is full of pleasant activities with family, friends, pets, and nature."* A

CEO retired for a dozen or so years commented, *"My life is very, very satisfying. I have a great feeling of accomplishment, both professionally and personally with family."* A senior engineering management executive put it this way, *"My present life is comfortable, fun, intellectually and physically challenging, satisfying socially. It gives me opportunity to give back to others."* A Catholic priest who continued to work after his official retirement replied, *"I am an 'un-retired' retired person."*

Some expressed joy tinged with a little anxiety. A nurse remarked, *"I am trying to live each day as it comes, relaxed, and trusting God will help me, no matter what."* A physician, who no doubt has seen in others what he now experiences, said, *"I'm content, but life does get harder as you age."* Another respondent whose plans were changed when he became a fulltime caregiver for his wife commented, *"I am content...and I am reluctant to tell God how to run the world."*

Many approached retirement with anxiety; most worried about adequate financing, whether their money would last, if their investments would perform well. A healthcare professional expressed well the thoughts of many, *"My worries have always been financial, especially since the stock market has been so volatile."* A nurse noted, *"I worried about finances, since my income would be a third of my working income."* A physician commented, *"I'd be devastated if I became a financial burden on my children."* Another retiree, *"I pray the good Lord takes me home before I require any assistance."*

Others spoke of the loss of friends and position. A physician dedicated for years to the service of others said, "*Sometimes I regret that I am now taking away from others my knowledge and experience.*" A social worker remarked, "*Yes, of course I was concerned about a variety of things—Would I have enough money? Would I be bored? Would I miss my coworkers? And on and on.*" An educational researcher identified a critical worry: "*Could my husband, who retired at the same time, could he and I spend whole days together?*" Another educator said, "*I know I'm going to miss the intellectual stimulation of my peers.*" A medical doctor expressed a concern I have heard several times: "*I noticed that most of my colleagues seemed to die or lose their spouse within a year or two of retirement, and was concerned this might happen to us. So I was motivated to retire as soon as we could afford it.*" A single person expressed the worry about being disabled and money running out. A professor said, "*I worried about uncontrollable and dramatic increases in expenses—taxes, healthcare costs, and insurance premiums.*"

Even during retirement many live each day with fears that are part of everyone's life but which increase in retirement years. While many of these fears intensify in later retirement, they are there from the beginning for many. Maintaining good health and being self-sufficient are special concerns, knowing that declining health brings all kinds of other worries: lack of control, of freedom, of dignity, as well as being a burden to others or draining resources. For some, there is the constant nagging fear that they will run out of energy, be compelled to give up on the dreams for which they planned, and maybe need to give up their home, no longer able to look after it.

One respondent from Virginia expressed fear that her own dreams would be disappointing. A former director of social programs noted, *"I am aware of the passage of time and feel more pressure to use it in ways that are important to me and to the people I care about."* Another respondent stated, *"I fear not having the physical stamina to do some of the things I dreamed of doing."* Another retiree simply said, *"I am concerned about my wife's pain and weakness and my inability to help her."* A teacher put into words the common fear of us all: *"Since a goodly number of contemporaries have passed on, the knowledge that Sister Death will come calling one of these days is never too far from one's mind."* Some experienced this fear even more intensely when they thought not of their own passing, but of their spouse's.

On the other hand, some approached retirement without worry. One said, *"No. I never worried about retiring. I've never lacked for things to do."* An artist bluntly said, *"Worrying about retirement never entered my mind."* A woman who had been self-employed for years: *"I did not worry. Our whole working life was geared to support ourselves when we retired. We invested most of our income in real assets to prepare for this time."* Some people could live their retirement without fear, in a peaceful, confident abandonment to life and to God. Several simply wrote that they had no fears.

Worries there were for many, in abundance for some. Some looked forward to retirement and others hated it. Many retirees found a lot of satisfaction in their retirement years. Several wrote of their pleasure in being free to plan their own schedules and in having the flexibility to change them if they wished to do so. Spending time with family and friends was a delight to others.

A broker expressed the feelings of others who spent years in people-centered jobs: *"I enjoy having more control of my time and not having to deal with people in stressful circumstances."* An emergency room physician put his reactions simply: *"No night calls, I can sleep."* This same idea of control of one's time came across in another comment: *"I've always lived on a schedule with fixed objectives. Now I set my own objectives when I'm ready."* Another respondent said, *"What I could only do on the weekends I now do during the week and on a grander scale."*

Retirees who were busy people enjoy *"having time for the little things, such as a good book, the gym, time to smell the roses."* An educator put it simply: *"I love leisure time and few alarm clocks." "The freedom to do what you want rather than what you should or must"* included, for several, working on a personal project, volunteering, exercising, cooking special meals, planning for a trip, reflecting, going to the beach. One person who had a very busy working life spoke of his thrill at being able to visit across the fence with a neighbor, and to read the morning paper from cover to cover. A real estate agent put a nice slant on this freedom, when he said, *"I enjoy the freedom to work on myself, on my relationship with my wife and with my friends, and on my environment and my home."*

Another theme came up a few times: *"I love being able to do what I wish to do and not feel pressured by a timetable. I also like the time to concentrate on prayer and on my relationship with God."* One retiree enthusiastically affirmed, *"I was born to retire!"* A good number found particular satisfaction in volunteer service of others and were quite creative in responding to needs they discovered.

Glancing at the variety of people's perspectives suggests different attitudes and concerns in approaching this period of life. But all had the courage to retire, to reflect on why, and to approach the next stage of life with peace and determination. Reflecting on one's retirement is a good start. We have seen various reactions—relief, loss, gratitude, freedom, and excitement.

Signs you are ready to retire

Your work no longer gives you the satisfaction it used to.

You are peaceful, even if not certain, about your financial future.

You have interests, hobbies, plans.

You keep thinking about retirement.

You and your spouse get enthusiastic when you discuss this possibility.

Signs you are not ready to retire

All your friends are at work.

You think of work all the time.

You have no life outside of work.

You feel you have to be productive.

You are afraid to retire.

Opportunities Retirement Offers

The meaning of life is not found in what you do but who you are. Working life is often pressure to do, to serve, to contribute, and to produce. However, you do not have to justify retirement by telling people that you are trying be useful. Several say it is the best decision they ever made. Others regret delaying their retirement. Many just say they love it. Previously, one retired from work to enter into the golden years of rest. Now, you retire from a job into life's busiest period of creative work and enjoyment. You may no longer be employed, but you might have lots of work.

After years when other people had claims on your time, it is a delightful change to be in control of one's time. You can get up when you wish, rest if you so choose, and do those things you always wanted to do. Remember how you would say that you would like to do this or that, if only you had the time? Now you have the time! A woman from Washington State, retired for just a few years, expressed delight in now having time to visit with friends, to attend to grandchildren's activities, to take rides to enjoy the countryside and wildlife. Several spoke of enjoying more contact with their families.

Clearly, time needs organizing so that you do not just drift aimlessly. Some retirees are very busy with church activities, social community service, household tasks, and management of their finances. What I have found personally, in observing others, is that with a little prudent planning, both annually and weekly, time flies with interest, excitement, and greater meaning, and often there is just not enough of it. Of course, no longer being bound to a schedule means you can be flexible, change your mind, do something different, and even do nothing at all.

One woman observed: *"I'm feeling more satisfied about how I am doing things now."* A similar idea was expressed: *"I'm not doing anything I didn't think I would be doing, but I have more time to enjoy my life."* A nurse remarked, *"The pace of life has slowed down, the stress has been greatly relieved, and I now have more time for family, friends, and exercise."* I appreciated the insight of one comment: *"There's a sense of gratitude for my many blessings, and I have the time to be grateful."*

Many people's working lives are very full and sometimes pressured. Retirement gives you a different sense of time, meetings can be open-ended, and you can just stop to chat to anyone. Retirement offers the chance of quality time, perhaps like never before. Many still see retirement as the stage prior to death. But retirement itself includes several stages of its own, and only the last is a proximate preparation for death. The others are preparations for the life you were always meant to live.

Retirement gives opportunity for spouses to spend more time together. Many may develop new friendships, partners in sports, companions in hobbies, coworkers in volunteer services. However, quality time for you and your spouse is there like never before, and it can enrich your lives together. As one person indicated to me, *"Most men are unaware of the impact they will have on what has been the wife's domain for over twenty years. Chances are you will now be physically present every day, all day, in your own home. Both you and your wife will have to get used to that fact."*

One of the great opportunities retirement now offers is for retirees to articulate a new understanding of retirement. This can become more and more important as we prepare for the baby-boomers' retirement—the largest influx of retirees America has ever known. Retirement is now a new ball game and old rules no longer work. We will have to make up the rules as we go along. For people of faith, this new vision of retirement will include a focus on perennially important values, a sense of vocation, and a desire to permeate this phase of life with the deepest values of our faith.

A New Emphasis on Joy

A key word I would associate with retirement is *joy* or *enjoyment*. Retirees can look at joy in one of four ways (see Robert J. Spitzer, *The Spirit of Leadership*, Provo, UT: Executive Excellence Publishing, 2002):

1. They can find joy in personal pleasure and gratification. Such retirees focus exclusively on themselves and have no interest in anyone else or the common good.

2. A second group finds joy in personal achievement in retirement, as they did in employment. They compare themselves to others, always wanting to be better and more successful than those around them.

3. The third group is made up of retirees who see themselves as involved in something bigger than self and find joy and happiness in making a difference in other people's lives. Other people's lives matter to them, and they impact very positively all those around them.

4. The fourth group is made up of those retirees who find joy in unconditionally giving themselves to transcendent values, and with wisdom that can come in retirement, they pursue truth, fairness, justice, and unconditional love. This is a pursuit of God and a desire to give self to the call and challenge of God.

Interestingly, several respondents spoke of the thrill and joy they found in giving away much of what they had to family, friends, and the needy. Others spoke of their newfound joy in having time for reflection and meditation. Still others clearly discovered a new aspect of themselves in giving themselves unconditionally to others in volunteer work. Many find lots of joy without lots of resources, living very simply.

Retirement gives us opportunities to savor life and the people and events that we experience. This joy is a delightful aspect of retirement; it is an opportunity to be playful in a mature way. In retirement we have the time to be present to life in a new way: fully present to savor both the joy and the pain. We have the chance to be with people in compassion and love, to sympathize and to empathize with them. We do not need to rush from one event to the next, from one person's presence to another's. A retiree can be full of life and full of joy.

A manager spoke of the peaceful joy he found in no longer having professional responsibilities, another office manager expressed delight in no longer being tied to the phone, and a priest expressed satisfaction in having time, space, and lack of pressure. A retired physician said he enjoyed having the freedom to choose how to spend his energy. A nurse rejoiced in a growing freedom from the laborious aspects of working life. A retired engineer enjoyed organizing his house and life. Another spoke of a newfound joy in spending time with her sister. A professor and poet said, *"I enjoy the leisure to figure out things. I like to read and to meditate. I enjoy watching the waterfall in the garden while eating breakfast, and listening to its roar in the winter.*" This idea of increased reflection and mediation wove its way into many comments. One said, "*I now work in the 'ora et labora' ["work and pray"] fashion of the Benedictines.*" Retirees can enjoy other people's company like never before, and in the process enjoy each moment of life.

A New Sense of Discovery

In retirement, the spirit of discovery can enrich oneself or the community life shared with spouse, family, and friends. Retirement can be a time when some are more willing than ever before to take risks: reinventing themselves, doing unimaginable things, traveling to unheard-of places. Retirement is not a time to mourn the loss of the past but to celebrate the opportunities of the future. Professional development and family enrichment are ways of life for most of us, and they bring satisfaction and fulfillment. Sooner or later, the primary issue for everyone is that seen in the winning phrase that Joe Batten gave to the U.S. Army, "**Be all you can be.**" This means fostering a sense of discovery in oneself, in relationships with one's spouse, in connections with family, friends, and new acquaintances. In retirement one can give full attention to each moment.

The responses given in questionnaires about the new activities to which retirees had given themselves and in which they had found satisfaction are impressive. A real estate agent gave music lessons to young-sters; a priest became an artist in oil painting and loved to travel to show his work; a nurse spent lots of time in arts and crafts. One retiree gave dog-training classes; two learned to be gourmet cooks; another worked with youth groups. An east coast nurse said, *"I am becoming more politically and socially involved."* Some did part-time teaching, acted as consultants, served on advisory boards. One said, *"Now my creative endeavors are directed more toward self-expression through the visual arts, music, and writing."* Another took up photography and learned digital-darkroom skills. A professor and poet said, *"I find that jobs around the house and garden are enjoyable and satisfying. I love working on new projects and using different tools I have never used before."* A doc-tor learned to hunt, a teacher to fish, and a computer manager to write creatively. Several got into golf, com-puter programs, and e-mail communications. Many just loved to read.

Discovery means you leave something behind to search for something new. It may be a deeper insight, a refinement or broadening of skills, or something entirely different. The approaches necessary to discov-ery are the ones that make this stage of life fulfilling and exciting. A social worker expressed her desire for dis-covery: *"Prior to retirement I thought of new things I wanted to try, people I wanted to spend more time with, places I wanted to go to."*

The greatest discovery of retirement can be the dis-covery of God. This comes through reflection and a refocusing on life's meaning for us, on our role and destiny in this world, and on our mission in the will of God. Retirement is a time of synthesis, when we see connections we have never before appreciated and identify the hand of God in these stages of our lives. With time, reflection, and a new vision of life, we discover new aspects of our relationship to God that give meaning to the life we seek in this period. In retirement more than at other times, we find a restlessness that only a loving relationship with God can satisfy.

A WONDERFUL TRANSITION

Retirement can be a wonderful transition to the best of times and an opportunity for new retirees to present society with a different understanding of retirement. Retirees can capitalize on the opportunities that retirement offers in greater abundance than ever before. We have probably all heard too much on the worries of retirement. Instead, let us look at this new phase in life with optimism—enjoying our retirement and approaching it with a new sense of discovery.

Retirement is a time for us to entrust our fears and hopes to the Lord, and to make this transition in peace. We prudently see that the same faith values that have motivated us in life now become an integral part of this new phase in life. This is not a time to focus exclusively on self, but a time to make a difference in other people's lives. Let us approach this time with hope, joy, and a new sense of discovery.

QUESTIONS FOR PERSONAL REFLECTION

1. What do you see as the positives and negatives of society's views of retirement?
2. What do you worry about most about retirement?
3. What is your dream about how you will spend your retirement?
4. Who is a retired person you admire and why?
5. When you think about the life you were always meant to live, what still remains unfulfilled?

THINGS TO DO

- Celebrate what you have done with your life so far.
- Discuss with other retirees what are the best features of retirement.
- Plan your weeks.
- Do something you have never done before.

THINGS TO AVOID

- Avoid being with people who are always complaining.
- Avoid worrying about the future.

- Avoid doing too much in your first year of retirement.
- Avoid thinking too much about your past.

THINGS TO THINK ABOUT

- How would you really like your retirement to be?
- Is there a component of service to the common good in what you do?
- How would you like to change society's views of retirement?
- How would you like others to think about you as a retired person?

2 *Refocusing Life*

FOCUS POINTS OF THIS CHAPTER:

- Welcoming retirement as a new vocation to rededicate life to the Lord

- Looking back with acceptance, gratitude, and celebration, and looking forward with hope and peace

- Examining life and refocusing priorities to make this period of life a gift to loved ones and to the Lord

- Taking time to be truly present to self, to spouse, to others, and to the Lord

Are You Ready for a Change?

There are many reasons why people retire, some positive and others negative. It is important to know why you retired since the experience can influence the years ahead. For some individuals retirement is just the right thing at the right time. An educational researcher who wrote to me commented, *"Retirement is best when an exciting job is no longer exciting and/or when home and outside items accumulate."*

Some individuals begin to think the time is ripe for retirement when they get bored with their jobs, find less and less challenge in their work, and become convinced that their organization is going nowhere. They may be concerned about their own lack of satisfaction in their work. This can result from a change in top management, a loss of the spirit of the organization, a realization that most of one's work is meaningless, or the realization that they can no longer identify with the organization's values. If the opportunity for an early retirement comes along with an adequate severance package, such people may well jump at the option. On the other hand, people who find retirement forced on them may suffer pro-longed feelings of rejection, diminished self-concept, and even anger and resentment into all their later years.

It is important to choose the right time for the right reason, to choose that window of opportunity between too early and too late. No one should just drift into retirement; rather, a person should plan for it. People with a healthy self-concept who feel they have achieved what they wanted in the professional part of their lives, and who are at peace with themselves, can accept the changes that retirement brings. Whichever situation is yours, you can take it and make it your own, and let it become the basis of a new phase in life. One retiree pointed out, *"My first task, mentally and spiritually, was to make daily efforts to accept things as they were. Acceptance came gradually."* This new stage is a new call to become the best of what we are capable. Retirement is a vocation. People who feel they are in control of their retirement have the best chance of making it a success.

When people move to retirement from different situations, their preparations will be different and their needs for a fulfilled retirement will vary. Anyone can prolong the current situation that they are in for years, but for what purpose? Retirement is an opportunity to reframe life, to pursue a different dream rather than project the best of the present into the future. First, you need to decide if your finances are adequate for your needs. There are plenty of helpful books and Web sites to assist you in this work. Second, if you are married, your decision needs to be one made together for a new phase in life. If the husband worked outside the home and the wife worked as a homemaker, retirement must change both lives; it should not result in a situation where the husband retires and the wife continues as before, as a full-time homemaker, cook, cleaner, laundress, and so on.

You need to know whether you can handle change and make the radical decision to break with the situations of the recent past. Have you done this before? Can you let go and leave things behind and simply move on without looking back? Do you have the resilience to retire well? Do you know the core values that have motivated your life at every point and will probably continue to do so? What is the meaning of your life? Perhaps you could describe for yourself how you see retirement, or brainstorm together with your spouse or a friend on how together you see retirement. Describe it in detail and then stand back to examine it to see whether retirement is something you would like. Do you feel any excitement about the future you see? Does the snapshot contain the things that are and always have been important values in your life? Does the image you see have the power to create new realities for you?

Of course, deciding to retire is a risk. However, life always implies risk; risk cannot be avoided but it can be managed. When you think about accepting this change, remember that not only will you change but others' attitudes to you will change. In retirement, former colleagues at work will treat you differently and may even ignore you. Friends may not know how to relate to you in your new interests, and they may give the impression they have to find something for you to do to fill your time.

If life is boring before retirement, it is likely to be boring during retirement. If individuals and couples plan prior to retirement to make their life exciting, then it is likely it will be exciting in retirement too. To be ready you must have interests, individually and, if you are married, as a couple. Think about how you will spend each day—mornings, afternoons, evenings. What will you do on weekends when all week is like a weekend? How will you spend holidays and special times?

Planning prior to retirement and during retirement needs to focus on who you need to *be* and not just what you need to *do*. In some ways retirement is the continuing journey of finding purpose in life. It is an ongoing experience of personal vocation.

One respondent says, *"Concentrate on living and not on getting older or dying. In retirement I have come to see the importance of 'just being' and that it's not necessary to be busy all the time."* A social worker who had done all the usual financial planning added, *"Then I went on to consider what were the more important aspects of how I would live once I stopped working for the state and went on to work or live for myself."* Several emphasized the importance of not just breathing a sigh of relief at retirement but also planning to transition into something positive and meaningful. This means making sure you have clearly established priorities regarding what is important in your life. In this context, many have given more time to family, friendships, creative outlets, sports, volunteer work, and the understanding of their faith. See how thrilled you are about something you want in retirement and then find ways to achieve it.

Do You Have the Right Attitudes to Retire?

When recent books, workshop presenters, or media commentators speak about *a worry-free retirement*, they refer exclusively to financial security. You could have adequate financial resources and still be bored, unfulfilled, unhealthy, and depressed! These are not secondary goals in retirement and can themselves create a worry-filled retirement.

I admit that financial independence is very important, but it is not by any means the greatest feature of retirement. Many retirees have built a large nest egg with little idea as to how to use it to achieve the happiness and peace they hoped for. Nevertheless, without adequate finances most retirees believe their hopes and dreams will be severely hindered. Retirees need a *prudent approach toward financial matters.* There are several books and articles that give stories of individuals and couples who have succeeded in having a wonderful retirement in spite of what would be considered by many financial planners as inadequate resources. Many retirees have the attitudes and creativity that enable them to thrive where most other people would not.

One of the key attitudes for successful retirement is the ability to *live with ongoing change.* Of course, the word *retirement* is very unfortunate and means only "withdrawal" from active and perhaps, but not always, significant periods of life. Perhaps it is indicative of society's views about retirement that no language in Western culture has come up with a more positive or dynamic description of these years. Retirement is a major change in life, but it also is a period of many changes—changes in employment, health, finance, and home. It is a time of significant changes in priorities, relationships, and values. Change is simply a part of life, and dealing with change is our response to the evolving part of our Christian calling.

An attitude that can help the smooth transition to retirement is to always *look forward, not back.* The past has made us who we are, and so it is always a reason for acceptance, gratitude, and celebration. This is true for the ups and for the downs. At the same time it is the *future* of each day, week, month, and year that gives hope, challenge, new meaning, and purpose in our lives. No one needs to abandon the past, but we move on. Thus, most treasure the past and want to see some continuity, as they embark on this changed future.

So many retirees claimed their lives were full, and they were *enjoying retirement*. In fact, businesses have sprung up to respond to retirees' excitement in their new lives—businesses to support retirees' interests in travel, music, exercise, sports, and in new places to explore, new homes to create, new opportunities to serve others, and new lifestyles to foster.

When we are dealing with couples who plan for retirement, men are frequently more focused on financial security and loss of their job satisfaction; women are often concerned about their husbands' health and ability to adapt. As more women advance in their careers, husbands may well retire first and be homemakers while the wife continues her career. This gives rise to the need to be *gender sensitive to retirement issues*. Former roles may well be reversed or shared in different ways.

A needed attitude in retirement is *peace*. Each of us needs to be peaceful with ourselves and our changes, with our spouse and family with whom we now spend an increasing amount of time, with our past and its successes and failures, with our future and its sicknesses, tragedies, and death. We also need to be peacemakers, healing the hurts and divisions of our own past with spouse, family, and friends, and with the increased tensions of modern religious, civil, national, and international life. We need to be peaceful in times of uncertainty, doubt, suspicion, division, and rivalry. Retirees can bring their wisdom and experience to bear in developing peace of conscience and peace of heart. This attitude can assure a calm, optimistic living of the retirement years.

A further needed attitude in approaching retirement is *hope*. Looking forward with determination to make this next period of life the best requires energy, the willingness to tap dreams below the surface, the awareness of the need to continue to contribute and to make a difference in other people's lives, and the ongoing desire that others continue to be proud of what you do and who you are.

A distinguishing characteristic among many retirees I know is that some have an *enthusiasm* about this new phase in life. They simply love it. This enthusiasm about life enables them to keep optimistic, upbeat, and excited. It can be present even among some whose health is not great and among others whose resources are not exceptional. Life is good for these people, and it has meaning. It is interesting that many refer to their enthusiasm, a word that means "in God" (*en theos*) for they are living life fully in God.

People enter retirement with different approaches. They retire for different reasons, some positive and some negative. Some approach this period with fear, anxiety, indifference, or excitement. Many have hope and some verge on despair. These are years for which we must plan, remotely when possible, urgently if delayed. We should welcome this time with the right attitudes, and if we succeed in approaching it well it can be a very satisfying time.

Can You Balance Interests?

Retirement is a time of major change and experiencing it can be initially shocking. A key attitude for retirees is acknowledging that they must balance their interests, facing up to this new phase of life, and integrating carefully its many requirements.

SELF AND OTHERS

A key need of integration is between self-fulfillment and concern for others. A newly focused appreciation of self emerges in this period that is not related to past work or position or achievement. It focuses on self in each moment of every day with a new sense of destiny, a new network of friends, a new use of one's time, and a new appreciation of life. In retirement, one can be more playful, hopeful, optimistic; have a more flexible personality than in preretirement years. This is a chance for an individual to be at one with himself or herself.

Although anxiety might be on the horizon with aging and ill health, a retiree can learn to look to the bright side of life and evidence more optimism, hope, and resilience than in previous situations. This focus on self is not selfish. In fact, no one can truly give to others until he or she has accepted self. Only then can they reach out to others with a mature self-acceptance and freely share with others who they know themselves to be. The person who comes in contact with inner self in this period can then become available to others in their need; in fact, such a person can be qualitatively present to others in generous self-gift. This awareness often comes through conversation with one's spouse or significant others, through an embrace of the more reflective moments of life, and through personal integration of past experiences.

WORK AND LEISURE

You often hear retirees say they no longer work. This is far from reality. One business professional said, *"It seems like I'm busier now than when I was working. I'm sure that's not true, but I never lack for something to do."* I also heard from an engineer who thought of going back to his job, but realized he just did not have the time!

We do not retire from work but from a paid position of employment. Most retirees work very hard, many too hard. One of the key qualities we need in retirement is the ability to balance work and leisure. While it is true that we should have developed a sense of balance between work and leisure prior to retirement, many work themselves to death for a restful retirement and in the process lose the attitudes necessary to be a leisurely and restful person. This is important because it is the reflection that comes in leisure that gives meaning to work, brings insights to work that otherwise would not be there, and gives opportunity for creativity, which is never part of a harried approach to life. Retirees can work but should integrate leisure into their lives, for it is the balance between work and leisure that gives meaning to our contributions to this world. This balance can be achieved by purposeful planning of our days or weeks, so that we create rhythms of life conducive to this balance.

"ALONE TIME" AND RELATIONSHIPS

Every human being needs both time to be alone and time to be with others in friendship and community. An exclusive emphasis on one to the detriment of the other is unhealthy. Some retirees, having left behind their former friends and colleagues and the people-contact and camaraderie they offered, fail to develop other friendships or to become part of a new community. The resulting withdrawal and loneliness can lead to isolation and unsocial conduct that are greater threats to a fulfilling retirement than the lack of resources.

Studies on aging highlight the fact that the lack of meaningful relationships is a greater threat to the retirees' well-being than disease. Close relationships give time for friendship, time to share memories and experiences, and time to share at an intimate level, which is, after all, the essence of a deep relationship.

Those retirees who have strong relationships with family, friends, and community are likely to live longer than those without.

On the other hand, it is not necessary to be with others all the time, continually moving from one social setting to another. Lives that lack reflection are mere shadows of what humanity can achieve. Being alone does not mean being lonely; rather, it offers the opportunity for older, reflective retirees to integrate the values of life. Being alone perhaps with some music that pleases us and aids in fostering a quiet time, or possibly with a book of poetry, or of religion, or of philosophy, or maybe with a newspaper or magazine that focuses on some of the critical issues of our world—these ways can create an environment where a person can think seriously, integrate issues in his or her own life, and bring a quality of synthesis to life. This is where older people gain their wisdom. So, one of the areas to which retirees should bring balance is between the development of relationships and the reflection that comes in time alone. It is this reflection that prepares us for encounter with God.

PAST AND FUTURE

Retirees also need to maintain a sense of balance between the past that has made them who they are and the future that can make them into the people they were always meant to be. Looking to the past is not simply nostalgia. It may be that our memories of the past retain wounds that have healed imperfectly, of events that caused us harm, or of people who failed us. It may also be that we will remember our own failures, reexperience our own guilt, and confront a life that did not attain our own goals. However, the past is also a reservoir of goodness, of the effects of other people's love, of joy and happiness experienced over and over again, of the many transforming effects of God's love. We must allow ourselves to enter freely into the recesses of our own past and to savor the sorrows and the joys that have helped make us who we are today.

Memory, however, is never as powerful a motivating force as is hope. Besides looking to the past with peace and a humble celebration, we also need to look to the future that still offers us the chance for growth and fulfillment. I remember seeing a mug from a Hallmark shop on which was written, *"Retirement is the beginning of the life you were always meant to live."* Certainly, a great many retirees give the impression that they are just getting started.

A nurse from the east coast said, *"The journey has just begun and I am optimistic."* The future is not something coming at us, but rather something we can help create. If unanticipated obstacles come along, we can create a response to get around them or to integrate them into the life we want. Sickness may bring a life of ill health, but it does not need to affect our well-being, which is the best we can be in any given set of circumstances.

In the first chapter we saw how many retirees looked to the future with excitement, planning a new home or a vacation home, new relationships, a new and more generous service of others than ever in their lives, and new opportunities to do what they always wanted. It is the future that influences and motivates life during the years of retirement even more than in previous periods of life. Our ability to envision aspects of that future will be the source of the hope within us.

Do You Have Support Systems for and during Retirement?

Prudently maintaining or establishing support systems can greatly enrich the experience of retirees.

FAMILY

Most people spoke about the importance of family; several mentioned the increasing closeness of family members during retirement years. Spending time writing letters or maintaining contact via e-mail seemed to have given new life to family relationships.

A physician said, *"The ability I have to help my family and grandkids and contribute to their betterment brings lots of joy into my life."* For several, there was a rediscovery of the importance of family. One couple mentioned the need to work hard to heal past disagreements, and others again spoke of the increased importance of family encounters. Others found joy in the support they gave to children and grandchildren whereas some found satisfaction in organizing family get-togethers. A nurse related with evident satisfaction: *"My great granddaughter comes to supper and spends the night every other week."*

While some stressed the importance of remaining close to family, others liked some distance from the family and the ability to live their own lives. Now and again there were hints of wishing to avoid unwanted expectations from family: for financial support, for childcare, or for work in their children's homes or gardens.

The strongest family support came from spouse, partner, or companion who provided the deepest friendship and intimacy. Retirement is an opportunity to repair any part of the relationship that is broken, rekindle this relationship, and plan and live out retirement together. Two men spoke of the deep love and satisfaction they found in caring for their sick spouses. A woman who worked in real estate stressed the importance of support found in reexamining her relationship with her spouse during their retirement years and of working to make sure that both had the same objectives for retirement.

The developing of close family ties during one's retirement years is a key component of a healthy and mature retirement. It is not something that will happen by chance as most of us know from our own family histories, but rather something that needs time, dedication, patience, forgiveness, careful organization, and leadership.

FRIENDS

Friendship is critically important in retirement. Many retirees I have spoken with said they had many friends, old and new. *"I feel fortunate that I have many friends who are important to me. I am still in contact with people from my school days, many that I served with in the Navy, some that I worked with, and some I've met since retiring. The majority do not live nearby."* Several spoke of having between six to ten significant friends. One said, *"I have a small number of old friends and very few new friends probably because I haven't worked on it."* Another said, *"Our best friends whom we have known for over forty years are the only ones that are really significant."*

However, retirement does offer the opportunity to develop new friendships with people we have never met before but who have similar interests to ours, or possibly because we now have quality time to give to people, which we might not have had during our hectic working years. While some mentioned discovering new friends in new neighborhoods of new homes or vacation homes, a London city banker also pointed out that in some cultures older people tend not to develop friends outside of family.

Friendship is a sign of health, and the absence of friends is a form of "dis-ease" that can have negative effects on one's health like any other illness. Just like a tree has several rings, so too friendship has several circles. The inner ones are the significant friends who nurture our lives, and the outer ones are different levels of relating, each valuable and supporting. As we grow older, it is useful to have some friends who are younger; otherwise we are always saying good-bye to good friends as they pass away. Husbands and wives often have friends together, but often the friends are more specifically the friends of one or the other, and the partner does not always continue those friendships when his or her spouse dies. Some have even found long-lost loved ones on the Internet.

MENTOR-ADVISOR

At every stage in life it is beneficial to have an advisor or mentor, someone who can be a sounding board for your thoughts and a source of honest critique of your ideas—a wise man or wise woman who speaks the truth to you, gives you advice that you know is good for you, and challenges you when few others will. Maybe in earlier life you looked up to someone as a role model for you in your profession. Well, you now have a new profession, and you will again need a role model who has gone along this path before you or who understands the changes involved and can guide you, even though they have not yet retired themselves.

Wisdom is not easily found in our contemporary world, but it is there to be sought in significant, inspirational people who can help make the difference in the quality of our retirement. Wisdom is not education, nor intellectual ability; it is guiding insight into the best decisions we can make at a given time. Wisdom can be enriched by education, but it is essentially a knowledge that comes from the heart. A mentor can be particularly helpful in discussions on faith and end-of-life issues.

When we find a mentor, we know he or she is not motivated by anything else except a genuine interest in our future and our betterment. Along with the help a mentor can give, we should include the various support systems within spirituality and religion, which are mentioned in other chapters.

HEALTH, SELF-CARE, EXERCISE

One of our major support systems is the ability to care for ourselves in all aspects of health. Human beings manifest their inner spiritual values through their bodies. Consequently, self-care is an important aspect of maintaining ourselves healthy for our spouse, our friends, and God. Sometimes we know that during our working lives we live unhealthily; we are stressed out and harried, we work while eating a quick lunch, we do not get time to exercise, and we sleep poorly.

Seven Points for Self-Care

1. Stop smoking.

2. Consume alcohol in moderation.

3. Balance your diet.

4. Watch your weight.

5. Check important health indicators regularly—blood pressure, cholesterol level, and so on.

6. Get important annual tests, such as for bone density, breasts, prostate, colon, and so on.

7. Develop an exercise routine.

ARRANGING RETIREMENT

Retirement no longer just happens; rather we need to be prudent in arranging it and handling it carefully. There are many interests that we will need to bring into balance because exaggerations in either direction can lead to frustration. Furthermore, we need to be wise in establishing support systems for ourselves. No one is an island.

We need to maintain social and spiritual health as well as physical health. In addition, we need to foster support systems of family and friends, give serious thought to finding a mentor to guide and advise us through this phase of life, and finally take responsibility for our health and exercise.

QUESTIONS FOR PERSONAL REFLECTION

1. Can you handle change, and are you ready for a major change?

2. Have you dreamed of retiring, and what was your dream like?

3. What would you love to do, if only you had the time?

4. Do you look forward to your retirement, or do you fear leaving the security of your job?

5. When you think of retirement, what disturbs your peace?

THINGS TO DO

- Be peaceful about your retirement, whatever led to it.

- Make sure you and your spouse have discussed retirement together.

- Keep a budget and check how long your resources will last.

- Find a mentor.

THINGS TO AVOID

- Retiring without preparation
- Being too concerned about finances alone
- Letting others determine the challenges of your retirement
- Looking back in regret instead of forward in enthusiasm

THINGS TO THINK ABOUT

- What are the good reasons for being retired?
- What are your interests, now and for the future?
- Who are your real friends in retirement?
- Are you fostering in yourself the best attitudes for your retirement?

3 *Using Leisure for Reflection*

FOCUS POINTS OF THIS CHAPTER:

- Letting the increase in free time be an opportunity to focus on the values of the Spirit

- Opening self to transcendent values through relaxation and creative self-development

- Approaching retirement as a celebration of life and a rediscovery of perennial values

- Committing oneself to uproot false attitudes that are contrary to genuine reflection

One of the most welcoming features of retirement, according to many retirees I have met, is to have control over their own time. Having been overwhelmed by schedules, deadlines, and time restraints, many feel liberated in retirement, as they find they have lots of time they never used to have. The question is how to approach the use of this time. Some find it oppressive and return to full-time or part-time employment; others fill the time with all kinds of peripheral projects. One retiree who had thought through these issues remarked, *"What I really enjoy about retirement is the ability to have twenty-four hours a day on my own. I enjoy the time to be alone to think, read, meditate, or just relax without interruption. These periods of reflection offer me time to grow spiritually and mentally."*

The reality today is that many retirees have more opportunity for leisure than ever in their lives. Nevertheless, we do not necessarily see a development of leisure that leads to personal enrichment; often it is a pursuit of extra work in one's free time to pay for the acquisition of the leisure goods that the retirement industry offers. Those who retain their free time often do not know how to use it, and they easily fall victims to mass-produced, prepackaged leisure activities that do not foster personal growth. Many people who are now free to develop the leisure dimension of their lives find they do not know how to. They need new values, training, and skills. Those people who know how to integrate leisure into their lives are models of wholeness, and many look up to them today, just as previously they admired models of a work ethic. Such people who live a leisured approach to life are genuine witnesses to a healthy, balanced life.

Leisure That Does and Leisure That Does Not Enrich Retirement

A correct approach to leisure is a critical component of a fruitful retirement. In recent years, there seems to be three basic interpretations, seen either in books or in the way people live out their lives.

IDLENESS, CONSUMPTION, AND COMPETITIVENESS

The first interpretation sees a close relationship between leisure, free time, and relaxation. In the past, leisure was the prerogative of the rich who did not need to work. Unfortunately, for many, the increase in non-working hours has led to a fruitless mimicking of a previous leisured class. "Free time" has become a measure of social and economic well-being and can result in empty idleness or be filled with unproductive activities and quantities of so-called leisure goods. For many, leisure is no more than this consumption of nonwork-related goods, whether in their "work life" or later in their retirement years. This interpretation, which I suspect is the most common in America today, confuses the real pleasures of leisure with spending on and enjoying *objects* of leisure. This confusion about the real meaning of leisure makes many retirees turn leisure into consumption. Hence, there have developed many new industries around the new "leisure needs" of the retired.

This understanding of leisure does contain some positive insights, some of which are readily appreciated by retired people. As a public health doctor commented, *"I had always enjoyed working outside and gardening, and I saw retirement as time to expand on my 'free time' to do more of that."* This emphasizes the close relationship between work and leisure. The approach claims that leisure can be fully enjoyed only by one who also works, not necessarily is employed, but works. It stresses that there must be a balance between work and leisure for healthy growth. This understanding also affirms that leisure in the widest sense includes ease, rest, and amusement, and that it is not merely the idleness and boredom of free time.

However, this notion sees leisure as passivity or injects into free time the same attitudes required in work. There is no real change of attitudes or true rest. Some retirees who were competitive in work are competitive in their leisure, in the acquisition of leisure goods, and in the social image they portray. All this is work and achievement. It is not an integration of work and leisure, but a prolongation of working attitudes into the free time of retirement.

CREATIVE SELF-DEVELOPMENT

A second general understanding identifiable in the last decade is the equation of leisure with creative self-development. Leisure is not simply freedom from work and obligations. Such "leisure" can result in boredom, killing time, or filling time. Rather, leisure is freedom for growth and openness to one's inner self and capacities. It is an opportunity to pause and appreciate the wonders of the world around us and grow as human beings in the process; it develops a second wellspring of self-identity outside of one's job. It is an occasion to share while free of tension, an opportunity for exercise, fun, and release, and a time to stretch interests and revitalize the senses. A CEO from Portland, Oregon, commented at the end of his letter to me, *"I'm sitting by the pool with a glass of wine. The sun is shining. Life is good."* Leisure is the enjoyment of the natural joys of life. It is a time for celebration.

This second understanding of leisure is correct but incomplete. It certainly corrects the negative, passive, and at times stunting elements in the first understanding. In fact, this second one not only refuses to equate leisure with free time but requires that we give up free time to creative leisure, to create genuine recreation. It emphasizes the appreciation that personal development depends on the integration of work and leisure, and that it is the latter which leads to quality growth. Work contributes but only as far as it is "an outpouring of the spirit," in which case it presupposes leisure. A good friend of mine, a retiree, said, *"There's a good deal of 'work' for us to do on our home. But we love it and it is more like play."*

In this view, leisure is the activity in which a man or woman fulfills the deepest yearnings of his or her heart. The repetition of work does not accomplish this, but the self-discovery and self-development of leisure can. What is learned in the creative effort of leisure can then be integrated into one's approach to the whole of life. *"Retirement is a happy period because one is privileged to practice those disciplines which enlarge the mind and spirit in the face of ever declining physical powers."* This second understanding, in addition to accepting the need of nonworking free time for relaxation, implies a commitment to growth through creative self-expression and indicates the potential value of leisure for the enrichment of the life of the retiree.

ONE'S INNER SPIRIT

Further reflection suggests a third understanding, which stresses a close connection between leisure and what we now call spirituality. Leisure is not only free time, relaxation, and creative self-development; it is directly related to total human growth and therefore is intimately linked with enrichment in retirement. Leisure is an attitude to life that includes rest and creative self-development, but also the very personal inner spirit of each individual, which each individual must discover for him- or herself. Finding one's inner self and discovering what renews and reenergizes the inner self are significant on every level of a person's life: human, spiritual, and religious. An approach to retirement that merely brings restful recuperation after a busy career, while having no lasting effect on one's inner life and attitudes, is hardly likely to be authentic leisure. Leisure is the relaxation of free time, creative self-development, and a self-tailored approach to life that always enriches all of one's personality.

This third understanding presumes that leisure will consist of a broad sweep of values that include personal, family, social, community, and cultural experiences: all discovered, adapted, and experienced individually. Several books on retirement, including this one, mention many attitudes and qualities that could become components of leisure, but it will be up to each retiree to decide if they are valid for him or her. Any notion of leisure depends on the understanding we have of the human person, and for a person who is a believer, a humanistic approach to life that excludes the spiritual is not enough to ensure the fruits of leisure.

Rather, the total human development that retirees seek must naturally include the spiritual, and leisure is equally necessary at this level. For example, in the appreciative wonder of a restful enjoyment of the universe, the believer is open to values beyond self, to transcendent values, or to the divine. In fact, it is in times of genuine leisure that a person readies self for a conversation about the deepest values of human life. Thus, this third understanding sees leisure as the attitude to life that enables an individual to focus on the truly human and spiritual dimensions of his or her personal integrity and wholeness. For those retirees who have a religious perspective on life, the experience confirms that it is not in the distraction of work but in the relaxed concentration of leisure that faith explicitly expresses itself; leisure is reflection amid preoccupation.

Beyond the affirmation of faith, leisure is equally necessary to experience what we say we believe in; leisure is an intense experience in a cluttered life. Finally, leisure is necessary to nourish the faith we profess; leisure is nourishment in a stressful life.

LEISURE AND FAITH

God has always called us, as in the Sabbath commandment, to celebrate joyfully and thankfully what God has given us. We are called to pause and publicly acknowledge that life is a gift to us. Does our life indicate that we believe this? The faith of many, moreover, claims that God graciously gifts us with a wonderful life. Do we show we are grateful by enjoying it? We also claim to believe that God is near us, in us, in others, and in the wonders of the world. Only in leisure do we prove this belief by giving time to developing attitudes necessary to meet God. We believe we can experience God personally and in community, but does our faith show this to others in the life we live? Are we "working" tourists who look at everything and see nothing, or do we pause, appreciate, wonder, and praise God who, we believe, reveals self in creation? It is not by work that we gain insight into ultimate values, and it is in leisure that we appreciate that it is gift. Leisure is the corrective that puts work in perspective and shows forth faith.

For Christians the gift of faith is in a religion that has a distinctive characteristic: that the revelation at the base of Christianity is a person, Jesus Christ, and not a set of teachings. When we look at this person who is the content of this faith, we see him walking through the corn fields, fishing, camping, dining with friends, retreating by the sea coast, emphasizing the beauty of flowers, enjoying a wedding, entertaining his friends by cooking their meal. He has no permanent job, yet he calls people who are employed—fishermen, tax collectors—but who are able to look beyond their business to respond to his call; those who do not appreciate his call are the ones who have eyes but cannot see, ears but cannot hear because they have grown dull (Mark 8:18). Others are described as unwilling to participate joyfully in a banquet, because they have working reasons to be elsewhere (Luke 14:15–24). To those who answer his call, Jesus assures them, "Come to me, all you who labor and are burdened, and I will give you rest" (Matt 11:28).

Jesus' example and teachings challenge us to see and appreciate with the eyes of faith; to spend time with others in friendship and love, for he is present in their midst (Mark 18:20); to enjoy the gifts of nature and know that the world is full of God's love; to let our leisured approach to life convince others that we have truly found a treasure.

Genuine leisure culminates in the spiritual. In fact, when it runs its course, it ends in the praise of God. Work never follows that path, unless it is undertaken in a leisurely manner.

A leisured approach to life is a basic element in spiritual growth. Retirement is a time for leisure, for wisdom, for a focus on the true values of life. It is not surprising that many retirees rediscover values of the spirit, a profound rediscovery that can even be compared to a conversion. Conversion is not possible without a pause, rest, or openness; for the believer, not without an appreciation of who God is; and, for Christians, not without reflection on the cross and awe and wonder at the resurrection. "See that I am he." "Look at me and believe." "Listen to my voice." "Appreciate the works I do." See...look...listen...appreciate...all attitudes that need leisure. Retirement offers opportunity for genuine reflection and a quality of wisdom that is closed to hurried, incessantly active, "indispensable" types. "Where your treasure is, there is your heart" (Luke 12:34). At all stages in spiritual growth, leisure is essentially an attitude to life and hence can be present in very active people at moments of deep involvement. However, periods are necessary when leisure is more intensely lived and expressed; such times of leisure facilitate a leisured approach to involvement in periods of activity.

Behaviors of Leisure to Develop During Times of Retirement

To truly enjoy leisure, one needs to be content, in other words, at peace with oneself. A person needs breadth and balance provided by broad interests, satisfaction in what he or she does, a healthy approach to one's own life, and good support systems, especially friends who provide deep and significant relationships. There are many behaviors of leisure that all retirees can develop.

REST

Do not be afraid of just sitting down and having a rest. In your regular working life, you showed generous dedication to family, social responsibility, the service of others, and the constant consideration of others' needs, but in a moment's relaxation or reflection, you can experience something deeper. One respondent put into simple words the expression of several: *"I always find time for at least a thirty-minute nap each day after lunch."* So do not feel you always have to be doing something. You have earned a rest!

READ

Read something you will enjoy. Books do not need to be related to your former career or to planning for retirement and financial stability. Rather, read novels, poetry, or light material. A leisured approach to retirement also offers opportunity to read more about the major issues of politics, world society, philosophy, and religion than regular daily life during employment may have offered. Take advantage of this and also of the valuable gift of time for daily reading of something that you find inspirational, possibly poetry, or a philosophy book, or a religious book from your tradition, such as the Bible.

RELAX

Take a little time each day to make sure you are truly relaxed. If at times you find that you need help in training yourself to relax, then find the help, or follow one of the several sets of exercises that facilitate relaxation. Nowadays, many people cannot relax; they are dis-eased not because of illness but because they are always worried about something, and if you acknowledge a similar need seek professional assistance.

RECREATE AND RE-CREATE

Part of every opportunity for a leisured approach to retirement is the re-creative component of enjoyable recreation. No one ever grows out of this need. Without falling victim to a consumer approach to recreation, each one can identify an enjoyable pastime that never becomes killing time or wasting time but is a pleasant reenergizing new birth.

RETHINK

In a time of leisure you can pause, rest, refocus, and rethink some of the values of life. After rethinking, you may come to the conclusion that the way you previously thought is the way you want to think in the future. However, you might also begin to think differently. As a London city banker expressed so well, *"Retirement was taken as the opportunity to change direction completely and adopt a more rural lifestyle."* While you have the extra time and are without many of life's pressures, think things over, evaluating your approach to major issues in your life, whether family, social, career, or spirituality and faith.

REJOICE

During the moments of leisurely renewal, rejoice in who you are individually and who you are as a member of a family or community. Rejoice in what God has done for your life. Rejoice, too, in what opportunities and challenges lie ahead and in what the future can be. Make your rejoicing practical by trying to bring joy into other people's lives.

REFOCUS

A break of short leisure is an occasion to examine one's life, to determine what the really important values of life are. By reviewing which aspects of life receive our quality time, we can see where the real values of our heart lie. Sometimes we claim things are important to us, but we always assign them secondary time, thus showing us the values in question are nowhere near as important to us as we like to think, or we like others to think. So, examine your life and find out what is truly important to you, the quality movements of each day, the significant experiences. During leisure time, refocus, prioritize, and determine to give the best of every day to those things that you consider to be the most important in your life and in this special time of retirement.

RENEW

Renewal is one of the key concepts associated with all leisure. The person who takes time away from regular involvement can emphasize a single-hearted, single-minded commitment to the renewal of his or her life for self-benefit, but also for the benefit of a family or community. Each one should return from leisure totally renewed. Some people prevent genuine personal renewal by claiming that as soon as they have some extra time they need to work hard on this project or that. Such reactions are sometimes praiseworthy but often are blocks to the restful reflection necessary for a careful direction in retirement.

REJUVENATE

Leisure should be a time of rejuvenation. A youthful approach to retirement gives hope and enthusiasm to others. It is not linked to age. As a real estate agent observed, *"Never let the child within die. Never become so jaded that you lose sight of the youthful wonderment of life and the countless ways in which it can be enjoyed. In our retirement years we have the time and hopefully the funds to further explore our dreams."* Approaching a period of leisure and re-creative enrichment appropriately, one can develop new attitudes that lead to more integrated lifestyles that show a positive valuing of leisure as well as work. As part of this refocusing, people eager to get the best from leisure should rest, read, relax, recreate, rethink, rejoice, refocus, renew, and rejuvenate themselves.

Behaviors Contrary to Leisure to Eliminate During Retirement

Some individuals approach retirement with the same work ethic that they approach life. They work hard at their retirement, determined to get the most out of it. However, some attitudes impede the learning and recuperative experiences of a genuine leisured approach to retirement; the resulting behaviors of these false attitudes should be held in check.

NO COMPULSIVE ACTIVITY

First, a leisurely attitude to retirement requires that we decrease compulsiveness of every kind. Some individuals are compulsive about study, or exercise, or work; about preparing for the future, or managing their assets, or being the best in one area or another. However, during retirement it is not necessary that we do everything we can do. In fact, doing too much can become a block to the ability to truly obtain from retirement that healthy, total human enrichment for which we hope.

NO COMPLAINTS

Life is stressful; work we need done on the house is not done on time, equipment is faulty, many callers are nasty on the phone, and some people are irresponsible. If we do not challenge, criticize, or complain, nothing is remedied. But complaining can become overused and even extended to people and situations to which we ought to show forbearance. Challenging, criticizing, and complaining are so much a part of life, we find ourselves forced to participate in the system, but at times we can diminish as people.

During retirement time, we can check our responses to life and to people. The effects of unnecessary complaining are particularly severe when one is with family or a group of friends, especially the spontaneous ones that form around people with responsibilities. It is valuable self-training to examine the element of complaining in our daily lives and to plan to reduce it, thus enabling us to distance ourselves from some of life's stresses and foster a more peaceful approach to life.

NO NEGATIVITY

Linked closely to the spirit of complaining is the communal sharing of negative comments. It is never possible to have a group of people who will always be satisfied with what is done. In fact, national statistics indicate we should always expect at least fifteen percent opposition or rejection from any group on every issue.

Dedicated individuals who hold positions of responsibility have generally had to carry other people's burdens for thirty years or more. However, with a leisured approach to retirement time they do not have to carry anyone's burdens. Often we listen to someone's problem and determine to do something about it, but during retirement we have the luxury of not needing to do anything. Involvement in others' problems becomes a return to a working approach to life and should be avoided when it constantly leads to negativity.

NO OVERDOING THINGS

Leisure should not be too intense. Even prepackaged leisure, arranged by others or ourselves, rarely does all we could want, covering all issues on our agenda. Content is nowhere near as important as attitudinal refocusing. Therefore, do not seek completeness at the sacrifice of attitude. Retirees should avoid contracting for extra work. When individuals or groups request time, avoid the pressure of feeling guilty because you say "no." Rest and renewal are yours; you have earned it. Avoid turning rest and renewal into work.

During retirement decrease compulsiveness, complaints, communal sharing of negativity, desire for completeness, and contracting for work.

Strategies for a Leisured Approach to Retirement

Leisure will not just happen. In fact, many contemporaries have lost the ability to enjoy genuine leisure and need help, often counseling, to redevelop it. Hence, the increase in "leisure consultants," wellness workshops, life coaches, and clinics for harried executives. Prudent individuals with just a little unpressured planning can establish approaches to daily life that will allow a healthy component of leisure to grow naturally during the time of retirement.

CHOOSE THE COMPANY OF PEOPLE WHO APPRECIATE QUALITY OF LIFE

Put another way, avoid overly competitive people who always seem irritated or angry and who generally leave you feeling the same way. A sense of competition can energize, but people who are always competitive are unbalanced. Do not bring a pressured life into your retirement years. Deliberately slow down the pace of daily living, even planning for a little idleness each day. Do something different that demands concentration, possibly reading a book that demands your full attention, or a conversation in which you listen without distraction or interruption. In fact, do one job at a time, giving it your full attention.

TAKE POSITIVE STEPS

Add a little exercise to your day to help tone up your body and maintain a healthy approach to life. Walking is as good as anything, and fifteen minutes a day, especially in a beautiful environment that can lift one's spirits, is an effortless addition to daily living.

Think about yourself in a different way, starting a new self-concept that is not dependent on achieving career success and security. Rather, readjust your values away from the social pressure to conform. In reassessing your personal goals, ask if they are really worth the price you pay in time, health, and relationships.

Do something that counters the specific pressures of what your normal daily life used to be like. If you worked under deadlines, make sure your retirement has none. If you worked with machines, get away from them for a while. If you worked in a team, do something on your own. If your principal work was boring, do something creative. If you worked on your own, spend some leisure time with others.

Relate your retirement time to full life values, and do not make it just another facet of the day. Leisure can be creative of personality during the time of retirement. It is not important to get the most out of retirement, but it is important to get the best out of it. Enthusiastically receive the opportunity of retirement. Do not worry if the experience is not exactly what someone else achieves. Genuine retirement cannot be prepackaged.

Advantages from being enthusiastic about retirement

Allows more time for reflection

Provides the chance to foster new friendships

Opens one's mind to new opportunities

Helps diminish stress and foster healthy living

Leads to quality presence to others

BE READY FOR NEWNESS AND CHANGE

Commit yourself optimistically to the process of renewal and growth that can come in retirement, avoiding overexpectations. After all, the process is more important than the achievements. Renewal of attitudes and vision takes time and patience. When a person has a longer expected time for retirement, he or she should identify the priorities for such times. What can happen in this time that could not happen for you at other times or elsewhere? You do not need the most from this opportunity, but the best; this requires a reintegration of attitudes and values. Be open to whatever happens. Do not become worried because things do not fit into what you thought should be happening.

SEE OTHER PEOPLE AS GIFTS

Enthusiastically receive into your retirement the people with whom you may share your retirement. Let them be themselves without stereotyping them according to age, nationality, former career, or wealth. Enjoy other people, their friendship, and their richness. Then, you can all grow together. Avoid intimidating others with your past experiences, qualifications, job successes, and so on, and refuse to be intimidated by others. This requires respect for diversity: what is good for one may not be so for another; what is growth for one may not be for another; what is leisure for one may not be for another; what retirement is like for one will be different for another.

Developing a leisured approach to retirement can have a significant qualitative impact on one's retirement years. If a retiree can foster a genuine spirit of leisure, it will bring added value to all that one does. For further reflections, see my book *Leisure: A Spiritual Need* (Notre Dame, IN: Ave Maria Press, 1990). This chapter adapts material I used in chapters 2 and 7.

QUESTIONS FOR PERSONAL REFLECTION

1. What is leisure for you?

2. What are your negative attitudes that ruin the peace and tranquility of your retirement?

3. How do people you know contribute to the growth of your enjoyment in retirement, and how do some of them stunt it?

4. Which of the nine behaviors of leisure could you develop or improve?

5. What are your strategies for a leisured approach to retirement?

THINGS TO DO

- Foster genuine leisure in your life.
- Rediscover the values of spirit.
- Think about yourself in a new way.
- Relax and plan for relaxation.

THINGS TO AVOID

- Exemplifying rushed, competitive, working attitudes in retirement
- Pursuing retirement as if it were a consumer good
- Doing things as you always did them
- Too much TV, alcohol, passivity

THINGS TO THINK ABOUT

- Which attitudes do you want to embody in your retirement years?

- Which attitudes do you want to
  avoid in retirement?

- What are the deepest yearnings of your heart?

- What would you like to do that you have
  never done before?

4 *Nurturing Creativity*

FOCUS POINTS OF THIS CHAPTER:

- Letting retirement be a time to continue to grow in new ways

- Drawing the best out of relationships and family life

- Striving to enjoy and appreciate life and growth

- Developing retirement by keeping one's mind active through continuing education

Retirement is not a time of decline but rather a time for creative development. In fact, retirement years offer the best possibility for personal enrichment, growth, and self-development. It is a time of creativity and new ventures; a time to draw out of ourselves God-given talents left hidden for years. We can now become who we have always wanted to be and can do what we have always hoped to do. Retirement is an opportunity to give ourselves to God in ways we have always wanted.

Creativity—More Than a Paintbrush

CREATIVE RETIREES

I was surprised that, when I asked retirees if they were creative in the years prior to retirement, a fair number said "no." In fact, several friends and contacts that I know quite well, and know to be creative people, also said, "No, I am not creative, not really." Perhaps that is because we are accustomed to thinking of creativity as the work of a great artist, writer, or sculptor. On the other hand, several retirees looked back to their previous employment and did refer to creativity they identified in themselves.

One CEO said, *"I've been creative in manufacturing, in dealing with organizations, and in building revenues."* These I felt were an interesting group of activities that we do not normally associate with creativity. A health-care leader said, *"I've always tried to make work-related things more efficient and productive,"* and a vice president in engineering said, *"I've been very creative in resolving problems."* This same idea was expressed by another manager who noted, *"I have worked hard at bringing a community together to solve issues in creative ways."* One respondent whose answers often indicated his high energy level replied, *"I am always looking for new challenges and different ways to meet them."* A couple of respondents linked their former creativity to new ways of doing similar things. Thus, an educator remarked, *"I was always creative in improving my working environ-*

ment, and now I work on creative arts." Another had a hobby of building computers and designing programs that continues in retirement. Yet another said simply that he was creative in a variety of professional pursuits and continues to utilize the same gifts in retirement.

While some retirees are reluctant to refer to themselves as creative, we can see that others are not afraid to identify their creativity in manufacturing, profit building, lateral thinking, organizational development, and problem solving. Of course, all these activities can be transferred to retirement in the same or similar ways. Several survey respondents recognized a new creative phase in their retirement, referring to their involvement in art, crafts, photography, music, pets, and financial management, to mention just a few. Some even exhibit their art and thoroughly enjoy this new phase in their lives. *"Traveling with and for my artwork has proved a real treasure for me. Getting involved in art has been better than I dreamed. Just the freedom—not only to do the art, but also to seek ways to show and sell it—is great."* Creativity becomes an outward expression of something deep within each of us that some may or may not have had the chance to express in preretirement years.

Many contemporary books describe the lives of creative retirees, some of whom were creative in long periods of their lives and succeeded in continuing this creativity into retirement. Others, however, were not known for their exceptional creativity prior to their retirement but then flourished in their retirement years. It is a wonderful experience to read some of the books that tell us of the creative endeavors of gifted men and women who were exceptional well into retirement age or who brought forth their gifts only in retirement years.

NEW BEGINNINGS

The word *create* actually means to make something out of nothing. A creative person brings to birth something that previously did not exist. It could be an idea, a painting style, an understanding of reality, or a new form of poetry. It could also be a new interpretation of events, a new social or political policy, or a new expression of relationships. Creativity is an attitude and a process, but it is not necessarily identified with the end product.

Michelangelo had a way with stone and with paint that brought his subjects to life. Beethoven could do the same with the sounds of music. Galileo showed us a universe unseen before his revelations. Mahatma Gandhi made something wonderful out of nothing when he dedicated himself to nonviolent revolution. By calling the Second Vatican Council, Pope John XXIII opened up a church closed in on itself. All these creative gestures gave birth to something that previously did not exist. It is also true that there is creativity in comedians like Jerry Seinfeld or Bill Cosby, who showed us the funny side of things and helped us laugh at something we had never seen before. There is creativity in a Nelson Mandela, who found a way out of apartheid when no one else could.

There is evident creativity in the scientific discoveries of Nobel prizewinners, many of whom are of retirement age.

Is it not true that we love to see beautiful, inspiring, and original works of art, music, film, and literature? However, we also wish someone could come up with a creative solution to wars in the Middle East, to racial hatred in the Balkans, to religious differences around the world, to poverty and abuse everywhere. Even in our own lives, we may wish for a creative solution to a disease, to a family breakup, to a loved one's withdrawal, or to a loss of meaning and purpose in life.

We can speak of creativity in relation to an individual in his or her own personal life. In fact, an individual can rejoice in his or her own creativity when no one else appreciates it. We can also speak of creativity in relation to others, creativity that is recognized by society. Finally, we can speak of creativity manifested by groups who through their collaboration, or insight, or artistic ability create something together that each never could have done alone.

KEY COMPONENTS OF CREATIVITY

Creativity can refer to any aspect of our lives and can be found in anyone. It is essentially a new way of dealing with reality. It does not happen by chance, but it is the result of an inner renewal that is then shown outwardly. In retired people, creativity may be the transference of skills previously experienced in totally different situations. Some retirees' creativity may be the overflow of creativity from their working lives. In these cases, retirees were creative before retirement. Those who were willing to take risks, who could see many sides to an issue, who were constantly curious about things around them, who could appreciate the value of play as well as work, and who could waste a little time now and again, even in daydreaming: these are the people who may well transfer creative insights into the different situations of retirement. On the other hand, it may well be that the new context and environment of daily life in retirement becomes conducive to new approaches to life. These changed circumstances of retirement can become the impetus for new approaches in which latent attitudes and skills can come to the fore.

Creativity includes the many small breakthroughs in our daily lives—engaging in a new hobby, undertaking forms of work we never did during our employment years, creating a gourmet meal we have never done before, healing a family situation left unresolved for years, addressing social problems left to others during our employment years. Artistic creativity can also blossom in postretirement years, with former actors, business professionals, or teachers becoming extraordinary artists in watercolor or oils or becoming writers or poets. In every case we see something come into existence that was not there before. Creativity implies absorption in the process that leads to something new.

RESULTS OF CREATIVITY

Involvement in the many forms of creativity is very beneficial to older people. Whether it is in artistic expression, in social betterment, in new manifestations of one's love for others, and so on, creativity first and foremost makes the individual feel better about him- or herself. Drawing out of oneself qualities not seen before is energizing and strengthens one's self-concept. This then leads to healthy functioning of our physical life. Feeling better about oneself is an essential component of good health. Moreover, creative involvement of any form requires quiet time, reflection, and synthesis—all components of a restful, healthy, reflective, restorative life. When one's creativity is beneficial to family and friends, it gives added meaning to one's own life. People feel good about doing good, and its byproduct is personal enrichment.

Most forms of creativity are of service to others and can bring pleasure and satisfaction to other people's lives. This enriching of relationships has family, community, and social implications. Our creativity makes other people's lives better as well. People are thrilled to see a retiree developing skills never seen before. One of the benefits of creativity in retirees is that it is a witness to others, an example, and an inspiration. The teaching component of creative involvement becomes a model for others to imitate. When a retiree comes up with a loving solution to reunite estranged family members, it teaches others to do the same.

A difference between some retirees who seem to close down their lives in withdrawal and give up on living and others who energetically or quietly involve themselves in creative work is that the latter give clear evidence of having a sense of purpose in life. They constantly remind others that life has a meaning, and this can enthuse others in their approach to life.

Aids to Creativity

HOBBIES

Developing interests that have always been important to us can lead to added excitement in retirement. We have seen retirees who have dedicated themselves to things they have always wanted to do or do more of: photography, oil painting, cross-stitching, stamp collecting, crafts of various kinds, sculpting, following the stock market, gardening, and gourmet cooking. Some people like to think of sports as hobbies: golf, fishing, swimming, hiking, skiing, and so on. These hobbies grow out of real interests, they can become absorbing activities in retirement, and they can draw out of individuals creativity that otherwise would be lost. Moreover, these kinds of interest-based hobbies have a continuing educational component as part of their development.

Some retirees take classes to further their hobbies, and thus they stimulate both mental and physical growth. At times these pursuits take on a life of their own and become a source of income, and certainly a source of pride. I have frequent contact with an airline pilot who is now an internationally recognized sculptor, a religious minister who regularly exhibits and sells his oil paintings, a social worker who holds shows of her photography, a real estate broker who repairs violins, a manager who trains dogs, a university professor who finds her artwork absorbing, a teacher who has become a social and political activist, and many more. Hobbies can give enjoyment, generate pride, build on gifts that have lain undeveloped for years, and even lead to an additional source of income.

CONTINUING EDUCATION

Many retirees like to go back to school to get the degree they never had the chance to earn, to study something in depth that has always interested them, or simply to become the cultured person they have always wanted to be. Some go back to college partly because they enjoy and feel energized by interaction with younger university students. Others take courses on the Internet, linking up with some of the finest universities in the country. Many find that education gives them a new perspective on contemporary social and political issues, gives added meaning to their philosophy of life and their religious faith, and brings them new friends and a new identity outside of their employment focus.

Opportunities for continuing education are so common and so varied they can fit anyone's needs. Almost every town has opportunities for continuing education, extended learning, Internet courses, or regular daily or weekly classes at colleges or universities. You can generally create your own tailor-made program of studies and even design your own degree. Travel courses are also a great enrichment, offered through local high schools or colleges or through alternative structures such as Elderhostel.

APPRECIATION AND WONDER

We have all heard the advice to "stop and smell the roses" and know that in our employment years, we frequently did not. In retirement, we can take time to enjoy and appreciate the people and environments around us. The person who can spend time appreciating a piece of music, a work of art, a glass of fine wine, or a conversation with a friend finds that he or she changes as a result of the sense of awe, wonder, and appreciation found in the object of interest, actually seeing and appreciating something never noticed before. It might be a view in the countryside, the goodness of a friend or spouse, the joy found with a grandchild, the beauty of a favorite piece of music, an event that reminds one of God's love for humanity.

Genuine appreciation requires one to be still, to concentrate, to be inspired, to be silent, and to be receptive. These qualities enrich our moment of appreciation but also transform our lives, making us men and women who see beyond the immediate to the deeper realities of life, and who open our hearts to make contact with God. I have met many retirees who are among the most reflective people I know. They can be truly present not only to other people but also to a poem, to a religious ritual, to the implications of a social problem, or to friendships on the golf course. A sense of appreciation and wonder is an exceptional quality that brings creative insight to our understanding of reality.

KEEPING A JOURNAL

This is a great way to organize your ideas, your reflections on the day, and your insights into significant events. Journal writing helps you get to the essence of events in your day, stripped of the clutter of secondary things. It is also a method whereby individuals or groups perceive the core values of their lives and activities. When we cannot see the wood for the trees, journal writing is an exercise in wisdom and becomes a creative interpretation of life.

Some retirees write their own life story. This is also a form of journal writing, but it looks back over the past rather than focusing exclusively on the present. It is a healthy emotional process that enables one to focus on the meaning of one's life. It can be a therapeutic process as one enthusiastically sees one's successes in life or as one reflects on one's failures and maybe even the hurt that one has caused. In addition, it can be a healing experience as one puts into context the pains one has suffered in life. Often men and women just do not have the time to think things through; retirement is the time to focus on the essence of one's life, partly to celebrate it and partly to be at peace as one prepares for the next transition. In some cases writing one's life story or keeping a journal is also a community service as it preserves family history and community traditions, and even becomes a legacy for one's followers.

Who I Want to Be

The most important creative endeavor that involves each of us is to make myself the best person I am capable of being, the person I was meant to be, and the person God has destined me to be. This means seizing the opportunities for growth for myself, for others, and for the world. In some phases of life, individuals give the impression that their personal growth is achieved by imitating someone else, by having something they themselves do not yet have, by doing something they have not yet done, and so on. This seems to be a conviction that we grow into self by accumulating things, money, experiences, promotions, and the like. Thus, in this view, a person grows into who they are capable of being by adding on to life, enriching life, feeding and nurturing what they have with what they do not have. However, our real self is within, and we discover our potential by journeying inward and by removing all the false selves that society expects of us. Simply *to be* is a value; to be the person I want to be as God intended me to be is an expression of religious faith.

By the time of retirement, one has learned to know oneself well, and with retirement comes the sense of liberation to accept oneself with all one's strengths and all one's weaknesses. This emphasis on self-acceptance and the peaceful enjoyment of the present moment is also caught by another respondent who noted, *"Retirement at its best is joyous, spontaneous, and free in the way the activity of children is both work and play for its own non-utilitarian sake."* Being who you want to be releases unexpected energy. One retiree whose wife died soon after retirement says, *"In my recovery from pain and grief, I chose to answer the challenge in ways that were productive, life-giving, and beneficial to me."* One who is very active is pursuing his retirement goals mentioned this qualifier: *"How does my retirement help those I love most?"* The heart of healthy retirement is found *in* the heart, in the values of the inner self. That is why it is important to focus on your growth and development. The creative and enriching experiences of retirement contribute to the excitement that can keep retirees young at heart.

The creativity in relationships that can come with retirement not only refers to new relationships but also to new approaches and new depths in existing relationships. Several retirees spoke of healthier approaches to their spouse or to their children. Family became more important and several had moved closer to one of their children's homes. They spoke with delight of new levels of love for their family and excitement in the role of being grandparents. The grandchildren brought not only inter-est, commitment, and responsibility into the retirees' new use of time, but also a deep emotional satisfaction.

On another issue, those who, contrary to their hopes, had taken on the role of full-time caregiver to a chronically ill spouse found that it seemed to foster more patience, dedication, and compassion than they had expected in themselves. Along similar lines, there is genuine creativity in the efforts to heal relationships with spouse, with parents, and with siblings. These things do not happen by chance but require commit-ment, time, concrete gestures of goodwill, and lots of patience. Out of all of these efforts emerge new, often very satisfying relationships. Of course, not all efforts produce desirable results. One office manager said, *"Aging parents, in my case an aging mother, has had a huge, unhappy impact on my retirement and on that of my brother and sister. In fact, it has added a lot of stress and work."* Yet I have also seen this respondent and others give time, effort, patience, and love to struggle to make their parents' last years as good as they can. In doing so they have certainly brought out qualities in themselves that enrich their retirement years.

Re-creating oneself in retirement can lead to situa-tions one never expected. One may need to deal with a family that struggles constantly. How many retirees fre-quently make trips to family members whose company they simply do not enjoy? One cannot say that this effort pays off in changed relationships, but it is often the fulfillment of responsibilities we feel. Families sometimes show to each other the worst of themselves, and time spent together is stressful. This effort to maintain family connections with the hope of improvement is probably a good thing. Only each one can decide whether the effort put into this kind of situation is worth it.

Maintaining good relationships with one's adult children can also have its painful sides. Perhaps they no longer hold the values with which we brought them up. Perhaps they find no value in a religious tradition that is important to us. It may happen they choose to live with a companion without getting married, something that was possibly unthinkable to us. They may have totally different values from what we have about money, work, children, social and political policies. Yet we continue to grow through our interaction with them in these situations. Continuing to love, to always be there, and to not be critical keeps the channels of communication open. When all is said and done, we try to make our love unconditional, and retirement may well be the prime time to show this dimension of love.

Some creativity, in work or in attitudes, comes to the fore in time of change and adversity. In fact, a lot of creativity appears in time of crisis. The word *crisis* is a Greek word that means "judgment." Crisis situations are simply occasions to come up with a new judgment, different from what we may have made in the past. We may face all kinds of adversity in retirement, in relationships, and in other circumstances too, but each occasion can be an opportunity to bring something new to the situation, something creative. We will also discover inner resources we never thought we had. The combination of experience and wisdom that can be part of retirees' lives leads to creative responses to some unexpected situations in life.

What I Want to Do

Retirement is a wonderful opportunity, not only to be who I want to be, but also to do what I want to do. An engineering general manager expressed the opinion of many when he said, *"I enjoy doing what I want, when I want, and at my pace."* Another commented, *"Two days in a row are seldom alike."* These ideas of "no pressures, no timetables," "enjoying relaxation," and "being in control of my time" seemed uppermost in the minds of many. *"I want to explore places and ideas,"* said a social worker. *"I enjoy the time to figure things out,"* commented a professor. *"Having spent my life with books, I now enjoy working with my hands,"* reflected an educator. When asked what retirees do more of now than prior to retirement, the top three choices were reading, exercise, and hobbies. Those who had retired more recently also mentioned getting into learning about computers, especially using e-mail for family contacts and the Web for entertainment opportunities, including travel.

These retirees seemed to be taking a delight in a simpler way of life, and at other times it was the fulfillment of a long-held yearning to accomplish "those things I would love to do if only I had the time." The first phase of our lives is a time of preparation, whether in learning or in building lasting relationships. Then comes the time of professional development, achievement, companionship, and family. While many used to think that the third period was one of decline into withdrawal and retirement, old age and death, it now looks more and more like the third period is one of consolidation of values, a focus on living the way we have always wanted to, and the culmination of life. After all, it is in retirement that things come together, and at this time that one can tap creative abilities that were built up over many years.

In summary, many do in retirement what they have never done before, since they now have the time to tap their own creativity. Some leave the city of their employment and start a new home where they want to live. If they do not like it, they are free to choose to go back. They gather around them friends they choose and not just colleagues in a common enterprise. They oversee their days and weeks, setting their own schedules, changing them when necessary, abandoning them when they choose.

There are three basic features of living out our hopes and dreams. Human beings strive to *be*, to be *for*, and to be *with*:

1. People strive to *be* the complete human being they are capable of being. They should never give up on life or become satisfied with where they find themselves at any given point. Rather,

they are always searching for fullness in their lives, yearning for constant growth.

2. People strive to be *for* other people in service and support, never becoming selfishly turned in on themselves while neglecting their responsibilities to others.

3. People strive not only to be, and to be for, but also to be *with* other people in the development of human community.

Early education trains us to do this, and years of employment are years of dedication to these values. However, these ends are always with us and remain in retirement. They are never attained fully in any period, and so human effort and growth continue in retirement. We still strive to be, to be for, and to be with, but we can now do so with greater freedom, greater clarity, and greater focus. Attitudes we have learned are still with us; values we hold dear are still ours. Our philosophy of life is simply lived out in changed circumstances.

Some retirees have chosen to buy a boat and live in it, traveling from port to port. Others see the RV and perpetual travel—visiting new places and meeting new people—as the life they find attractive. Renting their home of many years and traveling with the income is not a bad idea for some, while others use home exchanges with like-minded people in other parts of the country or other parts of the world. Some can bounce back from illness and do as much as they are capable of, and others can gracefully bear the burdens of old age. Doing what you desire is linked to the circumstances of the time; it is relative to each one's conditions. It can be done by anyone within his or her own limits. It is the daily enriching of one's personality, a creative phase of later life, a participation in the ongoing creativity of God.

CREATIVITY IN RETIREMENT

I am convinced that opportunities for creativity in retirement are just as frequently at hand as they are at any other time in life. In fact, I find retirement offers occasions for creativity even more than at other times in life. First and foremost, retirees have the time to think differently, to act differently, and to *be* different, and many of them choose to use the opportunities offered. Moreover, it is unpressured time when one's mind is unencumbered by responsibilities and free to follow previously unchartered paths. Time is open-ended and in abundance, a luxury rarely experienced by most of us during our employment years. Retirees not only have time but also the opportunity to discern carefully, to critically assess alternatives, and to focus on what they choose.

This gift of time and clarity of focus leads to opportunities for synthesis, the ability to see things in relation to each other, to see connections and interrelationships that can bring insight, creative assessment, and openness to transcendent values. Moreover, one of the great gifts of retirement years—with its open-ended time, clarity of focus, and creative synthesis—is peace of mind, one of the most precious blessings we can receive. All these qualities come together to make retirement years great opportunities for creative involvement.

QUESTIONS FOR PERSONAL REFLECTION

1. How do you manifest creativity in retirement?

2. What kind of person do you want to be in retirement?

3. What improvements in your relationship with your spouse do you hope for in retirement?

4. How can you improve relationships with your family during this coming year?

5. What do you think other people can learn from you about living well?

THINGS TO DO

- Establish a program of creative activities you have not done before.

- Find ways to bring joy to other people's lives.

- Keep your mind active with continuing education.

- Be socially involved in civic and political life.

THINGS TO AVOID

- Rushing anything
- Letting past dimensions control future decisions
- Being the retiree that others expect you to be
- Making decisions alone without the input of spouse or companion

THINGS TO THINK ABOUT

- Who do you want to be and what do you want to do in retirement?
- If you could begin life again, how would you change your priorities?
- What is creativity for you?
- Can you do something now that you have never done before?

5 Sharing Wisdom and Experience

FOCUS POINTS OF THIS CHAPTER:

- Making the inward journey into one's own heart and asking what it is that can contribute to improve this stage of life

- Contributing to the well-being of others in some form of volunteer work

- Healing the hurts of life

- Living a value-centered existence focused on the essentials of life

Journeying Inward to Self-Discovery

In the depths of each person's heart and spirit, there is *a zone of goodness*. It allows goodness to show forth so that we become our true selves. Often we cover up that personal goodness by our own less-than-desirable conduct or by simply choosing false values throughout life.

In Europe during the years leading up to the new millennium, and in some cases in the years since, many of the most beautiful buildings in the world were renovated. No one thought of covering them with a new coat of paint. Rather, the workers sandblasted the buildings to rediscover and re-present their original beauty that lay under the grime of centuries.

This is an image of the call that each person has to become who he or she is capable of *being*. It is not done by imitating someone else, by adding a new skill, or by immersing oneself in the self-help section of the bookstore. Human growth is an inward journey of self-discovery—a journey into our own hearts where we find the best of ourselves.

This inward journey requires *reflection* and quiet time alone. Young people rarely make this journey, distracted as they frequently are by contemporary consumer society. Adults in their working years, whether at home in childrearing and homecare or at work in the demands of career and professional life, sometimes have a chance to glimpse the challenge of this journey and to make the first steps. However, it is in retirement years that an individual has the peace, time, and focus needed to make this journey or to bring it to completion. As a west coast physician put it: *"I enjoy the time to be alone to think, read, meditate, or just relax without interruption. These periods of reflection offer me time to grow spiritually and mentally."*

The inward journey may well begin with reflection on one's past life, the choices one made, and the *priorities* one chose. This is a process of looking at what we are proud of and also at what we feel manifested less than our best selves. It is a reflection that brings focus and clarity.

An educator commented, *"In retirement, regardless of what I do, there seems to be a greater clarity connected with it as well as a greater mystery."* In fact, several retirees spoke to me about a greater intensity in their lives. They thought more deliberately about what they were doing and chose what to do with greater care. As a business professional pointed out: *"I stress the value of directing my life to more lasting goals. Building a strong philosophical and religious foundation for my life will probably be of more help than many of the 'to do' lists I find in contemporary books."*

The inward journey brings to light *true values that one has lived out* or false values that unfortunately one has accepted. These values can be personal, social, or even societal. The bad values that individuals live are often values that are so common in surrounding society that they become the normal order of the day. They are accepted by everyone, justified by society, and even religiously supported. Reflection on one's past gives an individual time and opportunity to reaffirm positive values and to confront negative attitudes that may have been part of one's life. This careful scrutiny is part of the slow process that retirees use to bring perspective, insight, and wisdom.

This reflective journey to the center of one's being *requires time alone*, but it is not a lonely journey. In fact, it is best made with one's spouse, chosen companion, or friend. This deeper discussion may well be on politics, social issues, or religious values but it is part of the process of clarifying and maturing one's inner values.

We spend so much of life talking about nonimportant issues, but reflective retirees have the opportunity to focus on more important matters. This journey of self-discovery includes the practical focus on one's knowledge, life experiences, emotional experiences, and so on. It is a time of reassessment and focusing on the essentials of life.

This journey toward the discovery of one's deepest-held values becomes a *shared journey* with others and the discovery of that which we hold in common. In fact, it becomes a gradual appreciation of the best values held by humanity. It is insight into who we are, how we expect each other to live, and what we consider are the core values of humanity. This journey contributes to new ways of learning about life and values, and it becomes the basis of a wisdom that we can share.

This journey to wisdom comes from *stillness, inspiration, concentration, and silence.* The stillness that retirement brings, the quiet waiting that replaces the hurried and cluttered times of one's working life, gives opportunity for meditation and receptivity that prepares one for genuine insight into reality and brings openness to God. A retired person has the time to be inspired by people and things around him or her. In our hurried, contemporary society we frequently lose the ability to concentrate, to savor the joys or the sorrows of life. Retired people with whom I have spoken express happiness in being able to spend quality time alone or with others in moments of joy and sorrow. Silence seems such an odd gift in a world of noise. Quiet time is a form of emptiness that can be filled by a true understanding of reality, of one's place in the world, of one's call to life with God.

What is the wisdom that these retirees can bring to others around them? Age brings a *synthesis of knowledge based on experiences* that are intellectual or emotional. Over the years of life, one learns so much from a wide range of experiences that are both positive and negative. As they age, retirees get a clearer perspective on life. This brings an inner wisdom that they can also share with others in volunteer work—with family and friends in the work of healing and fostering love, and with communities and society in discerning essential values in the midst of so many insignificant concerns.

Volunteering—Sharing Your Gifts

Many retirees find an outlet for their many gifts in volunteer work. A volunteer is someone who enters into the service of others of their own free will. Volunteerism also includes the idea that the service is unpaid.

Many people want to serve others but at times no one seems to want their service. It seems volunteerism was their own need for fulfillment. Volunteerism can be a substitute for people who really do not know how to share their wisdom. When someone "needs to be needed," all kinds of problems can arise. Therefore, volunteerism should be undertaken seriously.

Clearly, if an organization accepts anybody, it is probably not a suitable situation for serious volunteerism. If you wish to be a volunteer, ask yourself why. Why do people need your service? What is it that you bring to this undertaking that maybe other people cannot offer? How do you select an outlet for your generous spirit? Do you have the needed training for the kind of volunteerism you are considering? No matter how well qualified you may be, you need to ask yourself whether an organization actually wants your services.

Some of the retirees with whom I spoke saw their volunteerism as "*a giving back to the community some of what I have gained in my working life.*" This could mean donations to charities, and it could mean utilizing for others' benefit the skills one learned in one's working life. Some will readily identify with the manager of a large real estate office when he says, "*My job was to help people succeed, and I'm still doing it now through volunteer work.*" He succeeded in transferring his previous qualifications, sensitivities, interpersonal skills, and sense of service to volunteer work on behalf of youngsters from the streets and others who lost out on education. Now he leads a new foundation in its creative response to contemporary needs.

Likewise, a nursing manager transferred her skills in healing, patient care, and compassionate service to helping in a parish nurse training program. Some retirees always included volunteerism in their employment years. A property manager exemplifies this understanding by remarking, "*I've always enjoyed helping people....My involvement with volunteer projects has increased since retirement.*" Another retiree, always known for his generosity and spirit of service, pointed out how age can make a change in our focus. He comments, *"I volunteer less now, but with greater intensity."* A couple of others for whom volunteerism had always been important sadly acknowledged what an emergency room physician said, *"I don't volunteer as I used to. Every minute of my time is given to the care of my critically ill spouse."*

A business leader told me, *"The service of others was very important to me prior to retirement and increases in importance with every year that goes by."* This retiree and his wife have become models for others in volunteerism, and they have also found a new phase of life in their volunteer work. Their work on behalf of poor families overseas has brought aid to so many. An Oregon retiree, a former physician and public health administrator, used his gifts in a different focus. *"I volunteer my services on committees and in the work of encouraging folks to step up to the plate with their ideas and criticisms of whatever the activity under consideration is. Give your time and service where you can, but understand that others have experience and significant input to make before decisions are reached and actions taken."*

Other respondents focused their volunteerism in a wide range of areas of service from board and trustee memberships to such action programs as Meals On Wheels, Clothes Bank, Master Gardeners, Foodbank, and the Freedom Writers Network of Amnesty International, and others. Some used the Kiwanis and similar organizations as a home for their volunteerism, and others the local school system for mentoring programs and the like. Many centered their volunteer service within church groups: visiting the sick and housebound, working on projects for the poor, giving time to committee work, even working together as deacons and deacons' wives. Clearly there are so many retirees who have the generosity and wisdom to share with others.

The following are steps to a healthy spirit of volunteerism.

1. A starting point is awareness that one has been blessed in life and has responsibility to share his or her good fortune with others.

2. The transition to volunteerism should be made slowly and given some serious thought.

3. A person needs to experience a genuine sense of call to the area of volunteerism he or she is thinking of. Volunteerism is not a way to fill your time for a few hours each week.

4. Individuals who wish to volunteer need to know that they are compassionate and empathetic. Needy individuals who receive volunteer services will quickly be put off by artificiality and a lack of genuine concern.

5. Each volunteer needs to approach his or her service with professionalism, and if necessary, find training in the skills required for this form of service.

6. As in all forms of work for others, volunteers should establish simple structures of evaluation of their services to maintain quality, to correct failures, and to respond to new needs.

7. In choosing a form of volunteerism, find something that is relevant to you and that utilizes your gifts. Do not choose something that under-challenges you, or you will not stay very long.

Not every retiree will find a niche in volunteerism. One such retiree, having looked over several options, commented, *"There are many others who can do this sort of thing as well or better than I, and they find more satisfaction in doing it."* What is important for every retiree is to be concerned for others and to have a desire to share time and wisdom with others. There is no need to create something new. Rather, we can all use our life's skills in new ways for the benefit of others, and volunteerism is just one such opportunity.

Healing Divisions and Hurts

An area where the wisdom of retirees is desperately needed today is healing the hurts of life. We live in a society that is polarized like never before. So many individuals and groups suffer from pain and hurt. We have dysfunctional relationships, dysfunctional families, and dysfunctional communities. Our communities show little sign of change and almost no hope of change from the top down. Rather, the healing and reconciliation our societies need begin at the grassroots level and percolate up through the structures, until the so-called leaders are forced to acknowledge that the maintenance of division and polarization will no longer work.

Retirees have much to offer this healing process from their accumulated wisdom and experiences. They know what has worked and what does not work. They have fought many of life's battles. Retirees become more conscious of the fact that winning an argument and losing the love of one of their children is a profound loss. They know that some of their own truths that they have pushed on others as self-evident are not. Retirees have the opportunity to be less self-assured, exclusive, and oppositional. They can bring healing and reconciliation to the divisiveness of contemporary society. They can be critics from within.

The first focus of a retiree's healing wisdom begins with asking:

- Am I at peace with myself?

- Can I forgive myself and live reconciled to who I am, while striving to grow?

- Do I joyfully celebrate my gifts, maintain self-confidence and self-esteem?

- Have I refused to be controlled by structures, problems, my past failures, or guilt?

It is difficult to bring wisdom and healing to others, if I cannot first show it to myself.

The second focus of the healing that wise retirees can offer is to bring forgiveness to those in the immediate circle of family and friends. An attitude of constant goodwill toward those close to us undermines the ever-more-common practice of faultfinding and blame.

- Has the family alienated or marginalized some of its members?

- Have some family members made different choices than the rest of the family and had to pay the price for it?

- Are there in-laws who have never really been made welcome in the family?

- Have some family members gone through the pains of divorce, separation, abuse, alcoholism, or other forms of dependency and never been themselves since?

- Has one or another relative never made it professionally or financially like the rest and been made to feel it?

Hurts arise in families for all kinds of reasons. In fact, some hurts are caused by family members. Criticisms, disagreements, grudges, and alienation can go on for decades. As a person gets older, and hopefully wiser, one can feel called to bridge the differences and heal the pain. An immediate response is a caring attitude that begins with awareness that others are hurting as much as we are. It may be something one wants to do before dying. It may also be that a wise person sees the foolishness of maintaining differences that have caused so much hurt. It may be that he or she perceives the power of love, of healing, and of reconciliation, and knows it is urgent that families build on such values. When a person can love one significant other deeply in genuine mutual forgiveness, then there is the possibility of extending this to others and to society in general.

The third focus of healing is the one in which retirees can become models for those around them of wise approaches to the solution of life's hurts. The retiree needs above all to be seen as a person who is trustworthy, who does not take sides, but who struggles to unite. This includes self-control over conversations, never giving the impression of gossiping or betraying the trust of others. It means establishing the reputation of conflict resolution that leads to win-win solutions for those involved.

By sharing the wisdom of life and experiences in the resolution of conflicts, the retiree becomes a person of peace, a peacemaker, by removing all forms of oppression in his or her own ways of thinking, speaking, and acting; by his or her nonviolent attitudes toward others, both individuals and groups. The peace that results from sharing wisdom requires trust, humane attitudes toward others, and a willingness to settle tensions, rivalries, and conflicts through negotiation and not force. It requires a spirit of dialogue, openness to differences, and a readiness to accept the legitimate interests of others. After years of experience, the retiree should know that anger, resentfulness, impatience, or exaggerated competitiveness produces nothing but harm.

Life's hurts bring pain and suffering into the lives of all involved. Pain can be dangerous but facing it can change your life from being selfish to being selfless; it can focus your attention on how important friends and family are to you; it can make you think of ultimate values, of God, and of the importance of prayer; it can cause you to live in a different way. Retirees can bring perspective to this healing process because of their own experiences. Retirees can bring healing to themselves, to family and friends, and to the values of society. They can remember so much, be in solidarity with victims of pain, and give time to others to tell their stories.

Focusing on Essentials

Many retirees express the deeply felt need for balance in life, for focus on spirituality, and for a return to essential values of humanity. Retirees today are more independently minded, more socially and politically critical, and more outspoken. They are less easily persuaded by mass-produced thought, less a commonly identified group than ever, and less likely to follow the crowd than at any previous time in their existence. Their lives and experiences have brought them wisdom that focuses on essentials to guide their choices in later life.

FULFILL YOUR POTENTIAL

Retirees can look back over two thirds of their lives, reclaim the best they have been, and be content with what they find. Failures will always be a part of life, and retirees who look back can accept them and be satisfied with their lives. This self-acceptance of the past, linked to a passion to be the best in the future, is a guarantee of healthy living. The wisdom of life confirms the primacy of *being* over *having*, and most retirees who have been the object of manipulation for years by our consumer society know that *having* does not guarantee happiness and peace of mind. Retirees can generally say to others, *"I have been there and done that, and now I choose what is best for me."* No one wants to be a living failure. Retirees can examine life and reclaim what they are most proud of.

LIVE A VALUE-CENTERED EXISTENCE

Many people never discuss their values. Yet the values we hold motivate us to action and lifestyle. We all need to ask the questions: "What motivates me?" "What do I basically stand for?" "What do I believe about life and my role in it?" These values are not imposed from outside us except in the case of hypocritical conformism. Following the inner values leads to integrity when a person is true to self, when actions match values, when convictions are lived out honestly, when there is balance between private and public life, and when there is unity between one's inner and outer reality. Retirees are at a time in life when they can more consciously identify the values they hold dear. They can live them out and pass them on in an ethical will.

JUDGE EVERYTHING BY THE MEASURE OF LOVE

One of the most quoted comments of the Spanish Christian mystic John of the Cross is, "In the evening of your life you will be judged on love" ("Sayings of Life and Love," 57). While there are many values that merit attention in human betterment, one stands out as more important than any other: acting because of love. This is a simple but radical test. It is simple because we can almost always give a straight answer whenever this question is asked. It is radical because we know that individually we are our best when we are motivated by love, and the world is always better when people are motivated by love.

When I speak of measuring everything by love, I do not mean the accumulated gestures of love that the consumer society expects of us—flowers for Mother's Day, gifts at Christmas, cards for special occasions. These are all valuable gestures, of course, but they do not make us into different people. The love retirees should evidence is the transformational love that leads a person to make choices based always on what is the most loving thing to do at the time. This is selfless, unconditional love.

CONTRIBUTE, BUT DO NOT COMPARE

Wisdom leads away from a self-centered existence to an other-centered existence. The self-centered approach emphasizes one's achievements, power, control, and positions of prestige. When others challenge this self-importance, individuals become jealous and live in the fear of failure, in isolation, and in loneliness. Wisdom leads away from this concept of self-worth to focus on something bigger than self where we can make a difference in other people's lives. Wisdom urges us away from comparing ourselves to others and calls us to move toward an emphasis on any way we can contribute to other people's lives. Wise people can review their lives and see that comparing oneself to others serves no purpose, but contributing to others' lives is a secure form of mutual enrichment. This is where happiness is found: in working for justice, love, and community.

BE WILLING TO SHARE YOUR STRUGGLES

Frequently, we share with those who are dear to us, our family and friends, our achievements, hopes, dreams, and values. Retirees should also have the courage to share their deepest struggles that often come as we grow through the various stages of life or when we find some of our values changing. Struggling to mature our notions and experiences of love, pain, rejection, faith, self-understanding, and so on, can give comfort and enlightenment to others who will no doubt face similar struggles in their lives. While this also shows your own vulnerability, it is good to think about a small number of major struggles that caused you anxiety and pain. If they are the typical struggles of men and women, then why not help someone who is dear to you to anticipate them and have at least the benefit of how you eventually resolved them.

PURSUE YOUR DESTINY

The most fundamental question of life is, "What is your calling, purpose, or destiny in this world?" This is a way we live out our fundamental, motivating values, and fulfill our call by God. It is the expression of who we are. These are not questions we like to ask ourselves, but we must do so: "What is it that you can do that no one else can do?" "What would the world miss without you and your contributions to humanity?"

Retirees have lived through so much, made so many decisions, and pursued so many goals. Some choices are integral to who we see ourselves to be, and others are not. Some decisions create our personality, and others do not. What is it about yourself that you like the best? What are you most proud of in life? How would you like others to remember you? There comes a time for everyone when they become passionately aware that what you do is not of itself important, but who you are and who you are intended to be is. This means pursuing your destiny, focusing on essentials, and passing by life's secondary issues in which you may have been immersed for years.

LIVING THE ESSENTIALS

Retirees can live these essentials, and their lives become well integrated and more focused. Hope, joy, and fulfillment are never exclusively pursued but are by-products of a life based on essentials. The world's great leaders may speak of their legacies and hope other people think they have one. A life rooted in wisdom takes care of essential values, allowing retirees to become men and women with a legacy to further contribute to their family and to society.

One of the great contributions to society from retired people is that they can share the wisdom that they have accumulated over years of experience and which they can deepen through an inward journey into the depths of their own hearts. There they can identify the deepest values of their lives and share these with other people in volunteerism, or in the dedicated work of healing and reconciling divisions wherever they are. Finally, retired people can become models of these values to the wider society by urging all to be focused on those essentially good values that embody the best of humanity.

QUESTIONS FOR PERSONAL REFLECTION

1. Describe what volunteerism means to you.
2. List the gifts you believe you bring to volunteerism.
3. List your goals in volunteerism.
4. Consider your motivation in being a volunteer.

THINGS TO DO

- Make sure every day has a little quiet time.
- Pause, reflect, and enjoy the fullness of every moment.
- Become a healing person for the many who are in pain.
- Develop a few deep friendships.

THINGS TO AVOID

- Becoming withdrawn into yourself in silence
- Blaming others for failure

- Comparing your life to others' as if retirement were a competition
- Identifying the spirit of retirement with the acquisition of retirement goods

THINGS TO THINK ABOUT

- How would you like others to remember you?
- How does your own experience provide insight into discussions of contemporary world events?
- How do you wish to help others during your retirement years?
- What is your destiny during these retirement years?

6 *Striving for Fulfillment*

Appreciating the Gift of Time

A NEW ATTITUDE TO TIME

In retirement your time is your own, and you can use it as you like. This is a wonderful opportunity and challenge. We can treasure every moment with deliberate intention. The Romans spoke of time with respect. *Otium* was the time spent in leisure activities and personal pursuits, whereas *negotium* was the time spent on work, or business matters, in other words, time that was not leisure time: *neg otium*. Likewise the Greeks referred to quality time as *scole* and busy time as *ascolia*—the lack of leisure time. In retirement, we can have the best of times because we have the best of time to live in.

In the ancient world, we find three other uses of the word *time*, namely, *tempus*, *chronos*, and *kairos*. The first is simply historical time that relates to historical events. The second is measured time that eats up our lives with its demands, as the Greek god Chronos devoured his six children to prevent them from inheriting his throne and bringing in a new era. Chronos gives the impression of consuming anything so that he can keep things the way they were. The third concept of time is *kairos*, which means the time of grace, of gift, of opportunity, and of blessing. Retirement will include the first two understandings of time, but it is primarily the time of gift, of blessing, and of opportunity for every retiree, whether they recognize it or not.

Retirees have a fresh approach to time: It is free time and leisure time. It is graced time and time for opportunities. It is free-flowing time. One retiree observed, *"I spent a lot of my life dancing to other people's tunes. Now I dance as much as I can to my own music."* Most of us used to be faithful to schedules; now schedules are there to help us when we want them. Our time is a span of hours and days to be and to become, not a time to do and to produce according to the desires of others. This new focus on time is particularly important in the first year of retirement. Unfortunately, many retirees do not take charge of their free-flowing time and fail to survive their first year. They rely on previous attitudes to time rather than enjoying the fullness of the present moment.

A NEW PACE OF LIVING

Retirement requires of us a new approach to daily living. Some individuals worry whether they will find enough to do in retirement. You should never just do something to keep busy, but find a new sense of doing, a new sense of accomplishment, a new sense of achievement that does not need the acclaim of others, and a new sense of fulfillment without material rewards.

Nowadays in Europe, especially in Italy, there is a movement that speaks of "slow living," "slow cities," and "slow meals." The people dedicated to this movement seem to reject those aspects of modern experience that expect us to rush everywhere, pursuing the fast life in the fast lane, stopping only for fast food. They want to slow down, enjoy life, and savor food and friendships. They try to give quality time to everyone they meet and to everything they do.

Living Slowly

Go slow, be quiet, slow down, and think about the quality of your life. "Slowness" is modern, and you will find it very quickly in Orvieto, the capital of slowness. There you can slow down and enjoy the time you have rediscovered in retirement. Slowness is a movement, a network of over a hundred cities in ten countries, all dedicated to the slow rhythms of life and to plans for well-being. They oppose fast food and fast businesses in their areas. They focus on bio-architecture and avoid invasive structures and endless traffic. To live in the slow movement means taking care of one's relationship with the environment, carefully choosing opportunities for local work, selecting courses and conferences that promote slowness, and developing modern technology-based industries that do not require heavy industries and polluting trucks to support them.

Slowness is a deliberate decision against the fast life, against the useless rushing around that gets confused with efficiency, against situations in which the rhythms of machines take precedence over the rhythms of people. It is a precise decision to oppose those styles of life that lead to the extinction of what is truly human. Italian now includes words such as *slowlife*, *slowfood*, *slowfit*, *slowsmoke*, *slowbook*, and *slowcity*.

People dedicated to this movement live well, live in appreciation of the environment, live in careful attention to the rhythms of their own bodies, live with a love for art and culture, live amidst architecture that fosters beauty and the uplifting of the spirit. People dedicated to slowness seek to become connoisseurs of life.

(Based on notes taken from an article, "Orvieto: La capitale della lentezza," in *La Repubblica*, 12 February 2005, 36–37.)

It is important in retirement to be open and receptive to what calls you, to what impresses you, to what moves you to think, to share, and to empathize with others. Sometimes the best that we can do is to simply wait for something to happen and make the most of it when it does. Can we become more sensitive to a significant event that seems to be a call or more sensitive to a challenge that appears as God's invitation to us to rethink and to refocus our lives? Whatever we do, let us savor it, whether life, music, literature, friendships, food, and all forms of sharing.

A NEW SENSE OF ROUTINE

The word *routine* refers to the practice of always doing things in a predictable way. During employment, routines can be helpful; at other times they can insulate us from our feelings of insecurity by providing us with a lifestyle that is too comfortable and that we can control.

Routines can be helpful in retirement, too, since they can give structure to our day or to our week. When retirees do not know what to do with themselves, each day becomes a drag, and they frequently end up with depression. A working day has its own routines, and a retirement day also can, and sometimes should, have its own. The key difference with retirement routines, beyond the fact that they are personally chosen, is their flexibility. You do not have to do any of it, can change in advance, or change at the last minute. It is your free choice to make.

Introducing some things that are different can open up new interests. Along this line, experiment with daily, weekly, and irregular schedules. If you generally go to bed early, go out to a late dinner or show. If you generally do not watch much TV, then find a program you have not followed in ages and give it a try. If there are things you used to enjoy years ago and then stopped, try them again. If you always vacationed in a national park, try a city. Most experiences that bring happiness to one's daily life cost nothing. Making a list of those things that do bring you satisfaction and joy can be a great stimulus to meeting your own expectations, whether in areas of travel, education, social and political involvement, reflection and prayer, the profound questions of life, home or garden work, and so on.

Certainly, routines can give structure to our lives when we want them to. We can establish all kinds of delightful practices as part of a day filled with happiness that cost nothing. Flexible retirement routines can be part of a successful retirement, helping us pursue fulfillment and success in retirement in a very different way from when we were employed. We can abandon former routines with no guilt and commit ourselves to a simple life, flexible and self-fulfilling.

Getting a New Sense of Purpose

DOING SOMETHING THAT IS WORTHWHILE

We have seen the advantages of long-term preparations for retirement and yet must acknowledge that many retirees make no preparations at all until they are retired. Each one can still search for the best retirement possible for him or her. One key factor is one's attitude to time and a second key factor is a new sense of purpose. We do not just retire *from* a job, but we retire *into* a new phase of life.

Even in retirement, or rather more so in retirement than in working life, we need to ask, "Is what I am doing worthwhile?" Retirement is still part of our search for meaning and a response to the call of God in our lives: "Does what I do matter to anyone?" When it comes to a quality experience in retirement, no one else is going to show us the way. There is no "one size fits all," or some prepackaged, recycled plan of retirement, as some financial advisors and retirement industry operators would like to suggest.

A retiree I met on the golf course summed up his own reactions: *"Some businesses not only think we are retired, they think we are retarded!"* It is up to each one of us to create our own successful retirement, to establish priorities, and to choose to do something worthwhile.

DOING WHAT I HAVE NEVER HAD THE CHANCE TO DO

Each of us can ask, What have we always been good at? What have other people always appreciated in us? How would other people describe our best qualities? These will be values that reflect the best of who we were, who we are still, and who we are always called to be. There can also be other values within a person that he or she still needs to discover—those untapped gifts that are an integral part of a person's lifelong dream. Each one can ask, "What am I good at that I have never had the chance to do?" It is in response to these last questions that so many retirees launch out into new vocations or callings.

Among respondents to interviews and question-naires were a couple that started social services for needy children; a real estate manager who started a foundation for street kids; a business professor and his wife who helped transform an entire region in Latin America through their family-to-family programs; a nurse who became an instrument for political change; a physician who trained others how to deal with complicated civic structures; and a hospital administrator who trained healthcare workers to deal with the spiritual needs of their patients. Of course, there were also artists, musicians, environmentalists, photographers, financial wizards, counselors, and teachers, to mention a few: all people who never did any of this prior to retirement.

PURSUING SOMETHING WITH PASSION

A sense of purpose grows out of the ongoing daily living of values that are important to a person. Many of these values will have found expression through life in relationships, work, and societal and political interactions. In retirement, you take the values you have always had and always expressed, add to them the hidden values you have always had but never expressed. Out of these two, there grows a program of action built on all that you cherish. If you do not express these values, you will always be frustrated and live with a sense of aimlessness in life. If you go with these values and this focus, you have found a passion you can pursue. It should not take over the whole of life, but it can give meaning to life. The passion that gives meaning to life contributes to the human community, capitalizes on higher values, includes service of others, and enriches oneself.

TAKING CARE OF BOREDOM

The frequently suggested threat of boredom is no greater in retirement than in any other period of life.

One colleague said, *"I get bored sometimes…but less than I used to in all the endless and fruitless meetings I had to attend."* Each person is responsible for their quality of life at each moment. Getting the best out of retirement does not mean that every day is wonderful, but simply that it is the best it can be, given whatever the circumstances. To get the best out of a day, we need to take care of boredom. If this gets hold on us, it can become a bigger problem than ill health.

Boredom is best dealt with proactively than reactively, making sure we do not get into it rather than trying to get out of it. The word *boredom* refers to feeling tired, dull, tedious, or uninterested. No doubt there will be dull times in retirement, but there was plenty of boredom for most of us during our employment years. A little boredom does no one any harm, but we cannot allow boredom to become chronic. Rather than talk about conquering boredom once we sense it, we should anticipate what causes boredom for each of us and plan to avoid the circumstances that lead to boredom. Never continue to do things that are conducive to boredom, like staying home all the time, going to bed early every night, watching TV for hours, and so on.

What leads people to boredom? More particularly, what leads *you* to boredom? Some people see various rhythms in life—some accelerated and others quiet and reflective. What is boredom for one is certainly not for others. What is it for you? Is it the absence of people around you? Is it the lack of others' appreciation for your achievements? Is it simply not having something to do? Is it monotony in your daily or weekly schedule? Is it being with the same uninteresting people all the time? You can respond to all these causes, and others too, by planning your life to diminish the presence of these causes of boredom.

Planning in retirement can be a helpful reaction to boredom and a contribution to an exciting retirement year. On the other hand, never take planning so seriously that you become unwilling to change. I think of planning as I think of a paper cup. The former is great to hold together the year and the latter is good to hold a drink. No matter how good either looks, both are destined to be thrown away and replaced with another plan or another paper cup. Once you have an outline of a plan, look at it and ask, "Is it healthy?" "Is it exciting?" Keep it specific and yet also open-ended. Make sure it puts more excitement into your life, and yet also gives you a chance to be spontaneous.

Respecting Your Age

STRESSING PREVENTIVE CARE

The fact of living longer not only challenges retirees to respect their age and not to close down life prematurely, but it also reminds them that retirement will not be over quickly. Rather, retirees need to respect their age in view of the expected long haul of up to thirty more years. Thus, getting the best out of retirement while respecting your age means a preventive focus. Retirees need to stress preventive care in matters of health, safety, mobility, security, finance, and insurance. This anticipatory approach to many aspects of life is not a sign of weakness or fear or insecurity. It is simply a required new attitude, like someone who moves to a large city and needs to be more conscious than previously of the environment around them.

When retirees challenge each other to act their age, they often say "use it or lose it." This can just as easily apply to the use of one's limbs, one's appreciation for good music or good food, one's ability to savor reflection and prayer, as it can also refer to one's mind and one's sexual activities. Keeping actively involved at all levels keeps the body and mind active, and this is always for the better. Eventually all of us will need to give up something that we can no longer manage. We should do so slowly, reluctantly, and only on a temporary basis at first, being always ready to go back and try again.

FOCUSING ON ATTITUDES

Age is primarily attitudinal, while based on real events that affect us physically. Often our attitudes toward age are influenced by people around us, how they act when they get older or sicker. Try to always have some younger people in your group of friends who can challenge you to youthful attitudes, open-mindedness, readiness to change, willingness to start over again. Retirees can peacefully act their age, knowing it is a time of opportunity, the beginning of the life you were always meant to live.

A positive self-concept sustains us throughout life, and retirement is no exception. A healthy retiree knows his or her own worth and is peaceful about his or her own centeredness. Such a person is well aware of their talents and continues to nurture skills through retirement. In fact, such people not only appreciate their own skills but other people's skills too. They can use their talents well into retirement and continue to find reinforcement when they use their abilities well. For such people it is enough to *be*. Such individuals do not have to be forever trying to prove themselves to others. A retiree who acts his or her age knows that only the individual can create a suitable retirement, but no individual is likely to do it alone.

FINDING A RECIPE FOR SUCCESS

Retirement is a unique time for every retiree alone or every retired couple together. It is up to each of us to find a recipe for success. This means planning carefully how to spend each day, each week, each month, and each year. If this sounds like a lot of work, it is not. Some people will no doubt plan carefully once or twice, and then things will just fall into place. Other people who are reluctant to plan carefully will probably creep into an organization of their time through a hit-and-miss program with which they can live. The latter can be frustrating; the former pays high dividends on the effort expended.

Think about what makes up a good day, week, month, and year. What would you like to do? When would you like to do it? Why would you like to do it? And with whom? Then just do it. Later, evaluate your day, week, month, and year, adding things that you missed out on and subtracting things you felt were a waste of time. Not everything will be equally satisfying, but when taken together a package of involvement may well be very good. Everything good has possible negative side effects, and every problem has a potential for good.

Some people's retirement will be more fulfilling than others, but we can all work for the best of which we are capable. We can manage our time carefully, identify our own purpose in life, and thus give meaning to what we do. Thus, we can build an exciting year that gives each of us and couples together a satisfying retirement. We should act with the maturity of our age and with a realization that retired people are still young enough to have full lives. The time when dreams were off in the distant future is passed. Now dreams are what we hoped for in the past and can now make real in the present.

Fostering a Spirit of Reflection

THINKING THINGS THROUGH

I do not believe that retirees can grow in fulfilling ways without fostering a spirit of reflection. Clearly, retirees need to think through things constantly—issues related to their financial security, their healthcare needs, their relationships with family and friends, their own desires as they prepare for chronic illness and death, and their late-life relationship with God. Whether they realize it or not, they are practicing discernment. However, discernment is essentially a religious activity, examining the pros and cons of a decision in light of God's will for us.

Life before retirement is cluttered with decisions, many made in haste, and many later regretted. Retirement is a time when decisions need to be made carefully, always with the awareness that it might be the last time we get to make these decisions. When we write a will, establish a power of attorney, or video an ethical will for our family, we should face these moments with great seriousness. These decisions embody something of ourselves and challenge us to think things through as never before. Even regular decisions made during retirement to build a new home, to travel, to enter a new relationship, all affect others more than during our employment years. In later life, what we do must be worthwhile, and we need to maturely think things through to determine how we wish to live in these years, how we wish others to remember us, and what kind of a legacy we wish to leave behind.

EXAMINING LIFE CONSTANTLY

We have heard so many times that an unexamined life is not worth living. In retirement so many of our attitudes are fixed; we are who we are. However, as we face some decline in our mental and physical abilities, we must not allow circumstances to control our lives. Wellness is our goal even in times of decline; wellness is the ability to be our best at any given moment, no matter what problems we face. To achieve this we need to examine our life regularly in the early phases of retirement, so that it becomes second nature to do so.

We hear of good friends, family members, and acquaintances described as thoughtless, uncaring, unloving, and angry in their later years. Sometimes we say, "How did things get this way?" "Why did so-and-so drift apart and become unloving toward each other?" "Why is this person or that losing out on the best period they ever had to be with their children and grandchildren?" For some friends and family we find ourselves saying, "There's nothing you can do. It's just too late."

Retirees should grow and be fulfilled, but many do not because they drift into mediocrity in self-care, in relationships, and in their relationship with God; they do not examine their lives to correct faults that everyone else sees. We are accustomed to interventions in the lives of friends with addictions. But retirees often let themselves decline in attitudes because they have no means of correcting their decline and no one who wishes to intervene. Days of retreat for retirees, for married couples who are into late retirement, for grandparents on fostering the quality of love that they should evidence in these years would all help. Organized reflection must start early in retirement, especially for couples together, examining attitudes to self, to others, and to God.

TRAINING ONESELF TO REFLECT

Reflection does not come naturally. Reflection is a skill that many acquire early in life because of the kind of work they have, or because of their involvement in religious issues, or because they read stimulating books, or because they love nature and find it inspiring. Others rush from one topic to another in constant superficiality and distraction. If we have not had opportunity to develop the skills of reflection, then we should do so early in our retirement years, because a retirement without reflection leads to disaster.

There are four components for reflection: stillness, inspiration, concentration, and silence. Each of these skills comes from ordinary events of each day. They come together in times of reflection.

First, reflection requires that we can be still. Each day we should have times when we just sit still and do nothing. We do not need to be rushing here and there all the time. Even a little rest after lunch can be a time when we gather our thoughts together in quiet time.

Reflection also requires that we be people who can be inspired; otherwise we are left with just empty quiet time. Can we enjoy music, art, nature? Can we give time to foster a sense of wonder and awe toward the great works of nature and humanity? This means savoring the things of life, spending intense time with children and their interests, thoroughly enjoying the joys of friendships and love. Some people eat, some feed, and some dine; some drink down a glass of wine while others savor every mouthful. We need to be fully present to everything we do.

Reflection also requires concentration, and this is something we must learn from simple events of each day. Can we give quality time to others, listen carefully to a phone conversation, give full attention to the stories of a child about the events of the day? Or do we need to always be doing something else at the same time; for example, "tell me your story while I cook dinner, or phone me when I have a convenient long cord or cordless phone so I can wander around doing something else at the same time." Genuine reflection requires concentration on the issues involved, and this quality is learned in the ordinary events of each day.

Finally, reflection needs silence, and this is not easy in our noisy world. Each day should have quiet time; it is critical for health and for reflection. Sometimes the inner quiet we need can be aided by reflective music. Reflection is not possible when our minds are cluttered with all kinds of issues. We can train ourselves in reflection by focusing on four remote preparations—stillness, inspiration, concentration, and silence.

Some factors that help people to reflect and pray

- A suitable diet because no one can reflect on a heavy stomach
- A special place where one feels undisturbed

- Adequate open-ended time, because you cannot rush reflection
- A comfortable posture
- Food for the spirit—good reading

Steps in an experience of reflection and prayer

- A phase of relaxation and silence
- A phase of concentration and awareness of the present moment
- A phase of letting go of cares and worries
- A phase of acceptance of yourself as you are
- A phase of forgiveness and reconciliation with yourself and others
- A phase of contemplation and focusing on life or God
- A phase of hope and intercession for self and others
- A phase of gratitude

GIVING TIME TO PRAYER

Prayer is an expression of our relationship with God. It often starts with many words, as we talk to God, often not giving God much chance to talk to us. It later develops into meditation, when we think about God, our many thoughts replacing our many words. As our prayer develops, it becomes more simple, and we need fewer words or thoughts to express ourselves. This prayer becomes what spiritual writers call "the prayer of quiet." *Quiet* is a Latin word that means "at rest." At this time our prayer takes on the dimension of being a time that we spend quietly in the presence of God; we understand that we know each other, and few words are needed anymore. The final stage is when our prayer becomes a time we set aside for God to communicate to us.

Prayer is a growing relationship of love, a channel for God's love for us and for our love for God. It never happens without a parallel growth in our love for others. Both require words, thoughts, presence, and attentiveness. If retirees have not prayed much in earlier life, or have thought of prayer as merely reciting words written by other people, then they will need to commit themselves to a systematic development of their prayer-life.

First, create opportunities for nourishing reading about the things of life and of God. Second, find a place in your home, in a local church, or in the countryside, anywhere that you find conducive to quiet reflection. In other words, find or create your own sacred space. Third, establish a specific time to give to prayerful reflection. Fourth, talk to God about important aspects of your life—past, present, and future—praying in gratitude or sorrow, in acceptance and commitment, in hope and in resignation. Finally, try to simplify your prayer, making it ever less dependent on words, and end in a quiet loving presence to God that needs no words.

There are many human equivalents to this in relationships of spouses, family, and friends. We can look at someone we love and without words communicate our love, sorrow, hope, and dedication. In moments of quiet, loving attention toward God, we can do the same. No day should pass for a Christian retiree without a centering of life on God, the divine will for us, and one's personal destiny in the plan of God. It takes little time but does require reflection.

CELEBRATING COMMUNITY WORSHIP

Statistical studies show that many retirees, especially men, have little interest in organized religion. Their participation in religious practices and devotions does not increase in retirement years, and increasing numbers are turned off by religion's constant focus on money, sex, and control. By the time reflective retirees reach their later years, they have made up their mind on the importance and value of the religious organization's teaching priorities and practices. However, all retirees, both those who continue to be enthusiastic about religion's outward components and those who have lost confidence, can come together in worship, annual cyclic celebrations, and common expressions of praise and worship. Faith and religion inevitably lead to a communal dimension; commitment without belonging is not possible in religion anymore than it would be in a family.

Participation in the liturgy and liturgical year can enrich our meditative appreciation of the mystery of

Christ. The liturgical celebration of the Word and of God's saving actions in history is both the culmination of life and the beginning of a new phase of life for people of faith. Communal worship capitalizes on the qualities that believers bring to the celebration; but through interaction with others in faith, communal worship also creates dispositions for those qualities not already present and brings them to fruition in mutual growth and practical commitment in the marketplace of life. Some religious practices can be an integral part of the lives of retirees.

Growth and fulfillment in retirement are just other ways of looking at the universal call of God to each of us to fulfill life to the glory of God. This includes appreciating time as blessing and opportunity, pacing life for depth and fullness, identifying a sense of purpose and call, and dedicating ourselves to what is worthwhile. It means planning our days, respecting our age, and finding a personal recipe for success. True fulfillment requires careful reflection, constant self-examination, and prayer.

QUESTIONS FOR PERSONAL REFLECTION

1. How would you like to see your retirement develop?

2. What do you like to do each day? And what do you wish you would do each day?

3. How would you like other people to remember your retirement? What do you hope they will think you have contributed to others?

4. What are you passionate about?

5. Which experiences bring you the most happiness?

THINGS TO DO

- Do something that is worthwhile.
- Plan for each day, week, month, and year.
- Establish a new approach to time.
- Do something you have never done before.

THINGS TO AVOID

- Being controlled by routines whether old or new
- Thinking retirement is "one size fits all"
- Living in retirement with no long-term goals
- Thinking of retirement as closing down life

THINGS TO THINK ABOUT

- What brings you happiness?
- How can you live slowly?
- What has always been important to you?
- What are you passionate about pursuing?

7 *Finding Spirituality in Retirement*

FOCUS POINTS OF THIS CHAPTER:

- Identifying the major spiritual experiences of life

- Focusing on faith and how it motivates life

- Reflecting on the journey of life to God and one's place in this journey

- Seeing ongoing conversion as an integral part of retirement

A refocusing on spirituality in retirement years is particularly appropriate because filling oneself with the best values of life is appropriately done when one is empty of other concerns. Retirement is an opportunity to intensify the best dimensions of one's life: those attitudes that result from deep experiences of faith, whether in oneself, in a significant other, in community, or in some social, philosophical, or religious tradition.

These reflections on the meaning of life can enrich life, especially when done together with one's spouse or important friends. This reflective process on one's spirituality in retirement gives rise to reactions such as that from a college professor who said, *"Regardless of what I do, there seems to be a real clarity connected with it, as well as a greater mystery."* Then again, a simple but profound reaction from an accountant, speaking of her husband and their deepening of mutual understanding in their retirement years, was, *"How good that we can grow old together."*

What do religions offer to the retiree?

- insight into the meaning of life
- a sense of belonging to community
- an understanding of right and wrong
- conscience formation
- a sense of mystery and awe
- a feeling of security and peace of mind
- an understanding of the afterlife

Becoming Your True Self

Spirituality refers to the human effort to become a person in the fullest sense of the word, to develop one's authentic self. This effort-filled experience has been referred to as climbing a ladder to higher levels, following a river as it winds toward its own mature union with the

ocean, or as climbing a mountain, but most of all as a journey that is filled with ups and downs but is satisfying at
the end. Spirituality is the ordering of our lives so that we
continually grow in positive ways. It embraces all of life,
leaving nothing out, and makes of us all well-balanced,
well-rounded, well-integrated human beings personally,
socially, and cosmically.

Spirituality embraces all of life, making sure that
every facet of life responds to the inner call to live fully
at any given moment. This implies that spirituality is all
about relationships—with oneself, with other people,
with communities, with the world around us, and with
God. It is the ordering of our lives so that the values of
the inner self shine forth in all we do. We can also
understand spirituality as life in the spirit—living in the
spirit of our true selves, living in the spirit of a particular religious tradition, or, for Christians, living in the
presence of the Holy Spirit. Jesus Christ said, "I have
come that you may have life and have it to the full"
(John 10:10; NIV); that is spirituality. Irenaeus, an early
Christian writer, said, "The glory of God is when a man
or woman is fully alive"; *that* is spirituality.

Spirituality is not some nondescript emotional feeling of piety and religious devotion; it takes as its starting point the concrete circumstances of our daily lives,
our lived experience in the world we know. It is a journey in which the best values of humanity—especially
faith, hope, and love—help give direction to life and
help one advance toward achieving the enrichment of
an adult personality. It refers to one's entire life based

upon decisions that show fidelity to the inner motivation of life.

Spirituality is a journey of faith in oneself, in others, and in the goodness of creation; for those who follow a religious tradition, it is a journey of faith in ultimate values and in God. However, it is at the same time a journey of authentic, unconditional love of oneself, of others in relationships, and of the world in which we live; and, for those who follow a religious tradition, it is a journey of love for the pursuit of ultimate goodness and for life with God.

No journey is straightforward and smooth; there are always ups and downs and temporary setbacks; there are frequently delays, diversions, and longer sections of the journey than expected. Sometimes, when we think we have arrived, we find it is just a junction leading to another section of the highway. Some writers insist that one cannot grow to one's full potential unless one can also accept emptiness. There are lots of experiences of emptiness in retirement, such as lost careers, lost status, lost privileges, lost loves, lost friends, and so on, and so we have many opportunities for spiritual growth.

The way we articulate our convictions, the process of self-actualization, is through decisions and actions based on decisions. It demands deliberate action on our part. However, spirituality is not just what we do but also what happens within us as a result of a faithful living of motivating values. Spirituality is reception, openness to outside influences, and, for people within a religious tradition, openness to God's work of grace within us.

Spirituality is also a realization of need. It means giving oneself time and space, never being afraid to be alone, never being afraid of the uncomfortable, unknown, and unpredictable challenges that come from all kinds of sources. It means not worrying about not being in control, but being always open to new challenges. That is why some people refer to spirituality as a vocation. A person feels a sense of call to live in faithfulness to values that have been important throughout life and have made us into the people we are and were meant to be. Such people feel certain about their place in the world.

Therefore, spirituality is not some esoteric aspect of life. It is the call to become our authentic selves. It comes to us at every moment of our lives and challenges us to live out the values we have judged to be essential to our identity. Clearly, spirituality changes as our lives change and challenges us differently in different circumstances; it will be different for married people than for single people, it will be different according to cultural heritage, and it will be different for someone in the twenty-first century than it was for their parents or grandparents. Yet, it is the only way we can fulfill the deepest yearnings of our hearts.

Spirituality can be described in the following ways:

- It is an awareness of or a call to continual growth in life.

- It refers to a life dedicated to something or someone bigger than oneself.

- It implies being clear about one's place in the world.

- It includes reflection or prayer in times of need and emptiness.

- It means being constantly critical of one's life and values.

- It is having the humility to leave aside the worst of ourselves.

- It includes the courage to develop the best of ourselves.

- It refers to the desire to pursue one's own originality in praise of humanity or in praise of God.

- It is an awareness of the interconnectedness of family, friends, communities, society.

- It is one's personal response to the call of God.

Living Perennial Values in New Ways

When religious or spiritual movements address the topic of spirituality, one of the common notions that seems to herald the beginning of spirituality is the idea of a conversion. For early Christians, this change of heart meant giving your love and desire to objects different from before—more loving concern for the things of the spirit than a possible former concern for things that were more selfish. Conversion means not only to change the focus of your heart but also to get a new outlook on life. For everyone, but particularly for retirees, conversion means refocusing hearts and refocusing minds.

Conversion does not just refer to any change but specifically implies a change that is morally, spiritually, and religiously better. It is a courageous commitment to high moral development. It is the beginning of a journey in which we commit ourselves to make choices always based on our inner values. Whatever the convictions regarding the meaning of life that lie at the core of our hearts, conversion implies basing our entire lives on those convictions. What retirees cannot do is drift in mediocrity, unfocused and uncaring, without purpose or mission, for this leads to a loss of their dedication to others and a loss of meaning in their own lives, with very negative effects on their psychological and even physical health.

Retirement is a challenge to live perennially significant values in new ways. The values that have motivated life are generally established by retirement years, and it is unlikely that someone can change all those values that have given meaning to their lives. However, we can live out the values in new ways. Looking back at the peak experiences of life when one has risen above the ordinary and has touched transcending values, a retired person can feel called to greater participation in values of spirituality, such as reflection, prayer, and ritual. Retirees who experience a decline of the body, and sometimes the mind can, and do, focus on a greater spiritual awareness. Perhaps the following perennial components of spirituality are among those that retirees can live out in new ways.

A SENSE OF CALL
TO CONTINUAL GROWTH

This is a component of every approach to spirituality. Many people spend years living this sense of call in a passive way—doing what a minister told them, checking off their fidelity to a list of topics. Part of the process of self-actualization is that this passive approach yields to a self-motivation that creates the mature personality. Many retirees rediscover this sense of call to continued growth.

AWARENESS THAT LIFE IS A GIFT

As one gets older and loses many friends to sickness and death, one becomes increasingly aware that life is a precious gift to be cherished. This can lead retirees to value life and especially the quality of life, both others' and one's own. Life is the gift, not the accumulation of possessions, experiences, or status, but life and health. This awareness calls for a receptive attitude to life, gratitude for life, and a joyful and celebratory approach to important moments in life.

PERSONAL RESPONSIBILITY
FOR MORAL CHOICES

We live in a society where change is rapid, profound, and extensive. Easy answers to questions of morality are rarely available to us, and mature men and women must make their own judgments of conscience about the ever-changing realities of life. Changes in business practice, politics, social development, finance, medical practice, and sexual issues are very rapid; what is ethical and what is unethical are often difficult to identify. Retirement itself, now as long as a third of life, has many of its own moral dilemmas, and retirees can enrich their personal growth through clearly focused moral choices, for example, in health care, in quality of life, in inheritance issues, and in end-of-life decisions.

WORK

Although retirees choose to be unemployed, they all need to work. However, the ordinary conditions of work can lead to personal growth and to family, community, and social benefits. Our attitudes to work are still important whether the work be home maintenance, volunteer service, or a share in others' projects. When we put our heart into our work, pursue quality in what we do, engage our energy and creativity, and do this for the benefit of others, then we draw out of ourselves qualities that enrich our personalities.

COMMUNITY

Another perennial component of spirituality that retirees can live out in new ways is a commitment to participation in community-building at all levels: family, church, political, and international. We have seen many examples of retirees who are healthily committed and willing to struggle to develop a greater sense of community in their families, in political or educational groups, and in movements for social justice and peacemaking. We have seen many who work in their churches or in neighborhood groups, building networks of like-minded people, even generating a sense of community through chat groups on the Web.

THE JOYS OF LIFE

A key characteristic of spirituality for retirees is a healthy approach to the joys of life. We are the only generation in the history of humankind that has two lives: a working life and a leisure life, and the latter experience of leisure and the joys of life to which it leads must be integrated in mature human growth. Particularly during retirement years, we give more emphasis to the good things of life, to leisure and free time, to time with family and friends, to the joys of sexual love and to new forms of entertainment, culture, health, and wellness. So, retirees can approach all of these as growth-producing experiences that enrich their spiritual journey and create memorable moments. Retirees can be youthful in attitude as they age.

REFLECTION AND PRAYER

In the last chapter we saw the importance of reflection and prayer. Retirement is a time for reflection on the meaning of life, on one's role in the world, and, for people of religious faith, on one's relationship to God. We do not become reflective people by chance, nor does this skill come with our first Social Security check. Every day we should have time set aside for reflection, because a reflective approach to life can guarantee a successful retirement, and its absence can ruin it.

THE SERVICE OF OTHERS

A further characteristic of spirituality for retirees is a dedication to the service of others. This service will include efforts to humanize our lives and societies, cultural and educational development, defense of human dignity and human rights, the pursuit of social justice for all, and the insistence on economic well-being. To serve others is a prime way of personal enrichment, and in satisfying the needs of others, one satisfies one's own need to reach out.

Exploring Spirituality with Courage

Forms of spirituality change over time. What was a peak experience in early life may not be so in retirement. Spiritualities designed exclusively by males are rarely suitable for women. Spiritualities for uneducated individuals are inadequate as people become more educated. So, as people mature, their focuses on spirituality change and new emphases arise.

- Daily prayers are not as important as fostering a reflective life.

- Occasional good deeds are not as important as a life of goodness for others.

- Self-denial and self-sacrifice are not as important as yearning for fulfillment.

- Being alone in withdrawal is not as important as being a person for others.

- Rituals are not as important as spiritual experiences and ecstasy.

- Accumulating more is not as important as building a life of hope.

The new approaches to spirituality still use perennial foundations that reflect the human spirit.

Some perennially significant aspects of spirituality:

- Spirituality is based on a motivating experience of faith and of God.

- Spirituality is rooted in the best values of your life.

- Spirituality concentrates on what is essential to the spirit.

- Spirituality emphasizes a sense of community.

- Spirituality reaches out in service to others.
- Spirituality includes a responsibility for justice.
- Spirituality is always open to the search for truth.

Some key components of spirituality:

- An emphasis on the simplicity and intensity of the present moment
- A focus on an experience that changes life
- A concentration on authentic, unconditional love of self, of others, of the world around us, and of God
- An acceptance of one's mission and destiny in God's call
- A generous commitment to transcend self and become other-centered
- A shared dedication to the common good for all people of the world

How can retirees explore a new approach to spirituality that is more appropriate to them in their third phase of life?

1. *Think about your own approach to life.* Would you describe yourself as totally unreflective, spiritually primitive, and fixated on your own pleasure or pain?

Would you describe yourself as yearning for something beyond yourself, as wanting to be more spiritually mature than you are, and as embracing values that transcend the ordinariness of life? Would you describe yourself as a person who yearns for union with God?

2. *Reflect on a particular peak experience you have had.* Has some experience ever stopped you in your tracks? Perhaps you have experienced something or someone that felt like being hit by a thunderbolt, and your life has never been the same since. Was this an experience of love, of sorrow, of death, or perhaps it was an experience you cannot explain. Was it an experience that opened you to transcendent values?

3. *Describe how you felt following this peak experience.* Maybe you felt unworthy of this experience, and sensed remorse and healthy guilt for past failings in life. But rather than being anxiously overwhelmed by the negative, you felt you could be more comfortable responding with trust and that a new direction lay ahead. Was your experience of something beyond normal horizons?

4. *Ask yourself if this was a moment of conversion.* Was this a change of heart and mind? Can you look to renewal of your life, focused on the values you saw in your peak experience? Maybe you gained insight into simplicity of life, into unconditional love, into the power of human evil, into the need for reconciliation, into human helplessness and the call to hope, and so on. Perhaps you gained insight into God's love, compassion, desire for your well-being.

5. *Contrast what preceded your insights during the peak experience with what followed.* At times a special experience can leave one with feelings of embarrassment and sorrow, a little overwhelmed by one's previous inadequacies and failures, or the experience can be transformative. In earlier life these reactions could have led to anxiety and shame or confusion. In later life these reactions can be laid aside with peace, as a person feels they are no longer important. Perhaps, some people will say that instead of feeling blame for their past failures, they only feel a sense of God's forgiveness.

6. *Savor and celebrate the great sense of gratitude for the life you have.* When a reflective retiree thinks over his or her life, especially concentrating on any significant, life-changing experiences, the result can be a sense of reverence, an awareness of unearned joy, and a peaceful and gentle approach to the future.

7. *Decide how you should now live because of who you are.* If some special spiritual experience has touched you, what are you going to do about it? Clearly, you can return to savor the experience, relive its challenge, and restimulate the way you felt. Was it an experience of love with your spouse that challenged you to show your love more effectively in your daily life? Was it an experience of others' suffering that called you to a life of alleviating the suffering of others? Was it an experience of emptiness and helplessness that you felt could only be eased by the presence and power of God? Was it an experience of family happiness that reminded you to constantly foster the growth of family life? Was it an

experience of world injustice that called you to dedicate yourself to working for justice in the world? Was it an experience of hatred and hurt that resulted in your feeling the need to live for reconciliation and peacemaking? Was it an experience of personal healing that called you to believe in something or someone beyond yourself? Was it an experience you cannot explain but you long for it again?

THE IMPORTANCE OF SPIRITUALITY

There is nothing more important for retirees than spirituality, which focuses on their fidelity to the inner values of their hearts and their response to God. These values come from peak experiences in their lives and motivate them to become their best selves. Some retirees will live out their convictions within institutionalized religion, others in nontraditional community experiences, but the majority will take personal responsibility to find the means and supports to spiritual life wherever seems best to them.

Spirituality for retirees will embrace, affect, and color every aspect of life. It is that constant call to be more authentic in how we live and respond to others and to our world. It is a genuine abandonment to life and to God. As growth continues, we will face change that is evolutionary and often revolutionary in terms of our earlier life. In later life, roles are less important, but our deepest human qualities and experiences open us to the newer possibilities and challenge us to continual renewal of life.

QUESTIONS FOR PERSONAL REFLECTION

1. What are the most important beliefs you cherish?

2. How would you describe the meaning of your life?

3. Have you ever had a conversion within a religious framework, and can you describe it?

4. Do you ever pray? If so, why? If not, why not?

5. What do you consider to be the strengths and weaknesses of organized religion?

THINGS TO DO

- Spend some time each day in quiet reflection or prayer.

- Nourish your life with good reading.

- Accept personal responsibility for moral choices.

- Identify new values you wish to be part of your life.

THINGS TO AVOID

- Filling your time with busy work
- Thinking that life is in decline because your body may be in decline
- Feeling burdened by past failures
- Closing the door on your call to continuing growth in values of the spirit

THINGS TO THINK ABOUT

- The importance of religion in your life
- The best qualities of your life
- The meaning of life
- Retirement as a conversion, a change of direction in life

8 *Embracing Aging and Preparing for Death*

FOCUS POINTS OF THIS CHAPTER:

- Identifying the signs of aging in one's own life

- Planning ahead individually and with family for a careful management of future needs

- Appreciating the links between living well and dying with dignity

- Passing onto others the values that have motivated one's life

Experiencing Aging

RETIREES' REACTIONS TO AGING

Whether recently retired or retired for a considerable time, aging is a major concern to retirees. Not all respondents expressly addressed aging, but many of them feared the realities of aging, especially chronic illness, disability, dependence on others, and the possibility of becoming a burden to family members. While one does not just retire and then start to think of aging, awareness of the aging process gradually takes hold, despite some initial denial.

A physician remarked, *"I really didn't think about getting older and becoming physically less able to do things. However, as I have gotten older, I have become unable to do some of my favorite things."* Gradually one becomes more and more aware of the effects of the aging process. Another respondent said, *"What I was not prepared for was that the aging process was upon me, and my health has deteriorated to where mobility has become a real problem, so that realizing some of my dreams has not materialized as I would have liked."* At times it might be a different way of thinking, a sense of loss and loneliness, such as when a CEO commented, *"When I retired there was a sense of loneliness for quite a while. At first I was somewhat confused, getting up in the morning with no place to go, without a daily schedule."* A real estate broker said, *"I wanted to be able to travel anytime I wanted. The older I've gotten, the better it feels to stay home."*

Sometimes the first awareness is that things are just not the same as they were. A religious minister suggested, *"In retirement I have found less time than I anticipated, or it simply takes me longer to do tasks."* A property manager: *"I don't feel as good as I'd like. I am discouraged that I don't feel as well as I'd like, but I am blessed with overall good health. Chronic pain has impacted some of my physical activity; no more square dancing and fewer long walks."*

Those who planned for their retirement with excitement often found that aging and new health needs changed their hopes and plans, such as the nurse who said, *"I canceled the last two cruises I planned because of health reasons."*

Sometimes the pressures of aging and the increased illness become too much. A college professor noted, *"I have always been able to handle occasional illness and even chronic rheumatoid arthritis, but when bronchiolitis, pneumonia, and cancer of the prostate hit me in quick succession, I thought at times that I wasn't supposed to enjoy retirement, let alone have it."*

I have found that many just take their aging in stride and get the best they can out of life at each moment. One retiree noted, *"At times I get discouraged as we all probably do, but when one considers the alternative, you should hold your head high and do what you can within the limits that health imposes upon you. It just seems that time goes by so quickly that before I know it, another year has passed and another year has been added to the 'golden years.'"* Here and there was also a sense of humor, as with the man who had recently had prostate surgery: *"I may be impotent and incontinent but I am not incompetent."* Even when retirees can delay the outward signs of aging with botox injections, tucks here and there, hair transplants or wigs, exercise regimes, and so on, they still are aware of changes within.

AMERICA'S AGING POPULATION

America's population is aging. *"Most folks basically realize that retirement has its stark aspects. It tells them quietly that they are entering the final phases of life; that people judge that their best work is over; that they will be losing friends or spouses, which brings home the fragility and brevity of life,"* commented a former CEO of a national publishing firm. We might first realize that our friends are aging, then it dawns on us that we are too, and gradually we appreciate that we are surrounded by people who are also showing signs of aging.

Presently, 26 percent of sixty-five-year-olds can expect to live until they are ninety. These statistics will change considerably in the years ahead. By 2010, the first baby boomers will reach sixty-five, and by 2030, the last of them, meaning 20 percent of the United States' population, will be over sixty-five. Between 2010 and 2030, there will be a 7 percent increase in those over sixty-five, while at the same time there will be a decrease of 6 percent in those between eighteen and sixty-four. So the proportion of seniors to younger age groups will widen. By 2050 there will be 80 million people sixty-five and older in the United States. People will also live longer. In 2010 there will be about 5 to 6 million eighty-five years old or over, and by 2050 there will be over 80 million over eighty-five (*University of Illinois Report*, 2001).

People are getting older and living longer, with more fulfilled lives, and more opportunities than ever. The trend toward earlier retirement has halted, and more retirees are working part-time, a group that will certainly increase with the retirement of baby boomers. Attitudes to the elderly are improving as increasing numbers are seen to be quite successful in their retirement and in part-time work when they choose it. With healthcare advances, preventive medicine, increased self-care, healthier lifestyles, and attentive monitoring of diet, weight, exercise, blood pressure, and so on, many live moderately well into later retirement, with decline coming abruptly at the end. Retirees who handle aging the best are not those who constantly search for the fountain of youth, but those who enjoy the present and keep themselves at their own peak performance through reading, education, activities, interests, and enthusiasm.

THE STRESSES OF AGING

Stresses come from experiences of loss, illness, transitions, worry, conflict, financial inadequacy, and doubts and questions on a spiritual level. Some stress can be quite traumatic and negatively impacts a person's self-concept and security. Some stress is part of everyone's life and can actually energize us; dealing with a crisis or overcoming a newfound need can produce a sense of mastery. If too much stress becomes *dis*tress, then it leads to the usual effects of headaches, insomnia, loss of appetite, irritability, lack of energy, and depression, among others. It can also lead one to become selfish, critical of others, discouraged, angry, and full of self-doubt.

First and foremost, the stresses of aging are best handled by preparations that include the fostering of a healthy self-concept, the development of an expansive attitude to life, education on the growth stages of later life, attitudes of optimism and altruism, and the placing of our aging process in the hands of a loving God. These approaches get us out of ourselves and place the focus of life on others and our role in enriching life. Aging is not a new experience.

Besides these fundamental attitudes, retired people should maintain a good set of support systems made up of friendship groups, family groups, groups of other retirees, church discussion groups, and so on. In addition to support groups and the friendship and advice that come through them, retired people should maintain time each day for rest, quiet time, and prayer. This quieting of self is an excellent contribution to calmness and brings a sense of perspective.

PREVENTIVE APPROACHES AND SELF-CARE

There are often, but not always, responses to the stresses of aging. Older people can manage some stresses, but may need to accept others with no hope of change. However, responses that are important for us all are preventing problems and taking care of ourselves so that problems may not arise. As much as 70 percent of physical decline occurring with aging is due to modifiable factors such as smoking, poor nutrition, lack of activity, and lack of preventive tests. We can all take care of these issues and thereby reduce by 70 percent the decline generally experienced by aging populations.

CHRONIC NEEDS IN AGING

Retired people live longer than they used to and advances in heart treatments and preventive medicine have decreased some of the serious threats to life. However, living longer results in more chronic problems than people who formerly died younger used to face. Chronic disease management is now very important for two reasons: maintenance of quality life and protection of savings from constantly increasing medical costs. Among age-related changes, one can include heart disease and strokes, lack of mobility, and mental decline, including temporary memory impairment, sometimes delirium and confusion, and irreversible dementia, like that found in Alzheimer's: all these are becoming increasingly common.

In dealing with chronic pain, several professionals can contribute: the physician; the physical therapist; the chiropractor; the homeopath with knowledge of nature's healing; the psychologist or counselor who can listen and guide with understanding; the friend who acts as mentor or spiritual advisor who can remind us and be a standard of our values, philosophy of life, and sense of destiny; the religious leader who can bring guidance from a tradition's faith and teaching; and today's new therapist who brings comfort through massage and aroma therapy. All can contribute to healing, and all should be given a chance.

TOWARD HEALTHY AGING

Americans, who can expect to live longer, should also make sure that there is quality of life in the added years. There is no reason why getting older should imply that quality of life goes downhill. Certainly, we must maintain a positive image of our years ahead and not act as if we expect the worst. Those who think they are ill or are going to get ill generally act in that way. Rather, we need to proactively take personal responsibility for our health. Even with the added stresses and chronic pain, we can strive for wellness, which is the best level of functioning available to us at any given time.

In other words, wellness is as good as it gets at any particular time. Even someone who is seriously ill can be as well as possible for the stage they are in. Wellness is more than the absence of illness; it is a holistic concept that includes physical, social, spiritual, and religious components. We can work at wellness through self-motivation and healthy practices. Components of wellness include a positive outlook on life, personal care, a sense of purpose, respect and love for and from others, harmony with one's environment and surroundings, and a plan for balanced living.

Journeying with Grace

We must all deal with the experience of aging, manage the various additional stresses that we encounter as we age, and learn how to live gracefully with the chronic conditions of later life. Our challenge is to strive for wellness at each stage of life, living the best we are capable of at each moment. Challenges to continuing human growth and maturity remain with each of us throughout every moment of life; responding with care, responsibility, and dedication is the call of every retiree.

Aging is part of the journey of life, but for the mature and faith-filled, this part of the journey is above all a pilgrimage. This part of the journey is different because an aging person can often deal with life as a mystery that brings another kind of clarity. It is a time when a person no longer needs to compare self to others but can treat everyone with benevolence. No matter how powerful one has been or thought one was, a person can now be gentle, passive, and a follower of others' ideas and wishes. An aging person can journey with perspective; love is more important than obedience, compassion than negativity, wisdom than competence, listening than outpouring knowledge, and contentedness rather than restlessness.

This final pilgrimage is a journey toward the goal of understanding the meaning of life. It is a mystical journey in which the pilgrim is both looking at things in a different way and seeing things differently. In this pilgrimage, one no longer needs to dream of a perfect spouse, a fantastic career, a beautiful home. In the spirit of the pilgrimage, these issues are no longer in the forefront of thought and desire. Rather, there comes a point in the pilgrimage when this world can offer nothing else. One is ready for the next transition.

How one chooses to live in this world is ultimately determined by what one thinks will happen at the end of life. Suffering in one form or another is integral to life. Stages on our journey can overwhelm us, especially the moments of sorrow and pain. Even these can become part of our personal growth and in some way are bearable only when we understand them as part of the mystery of Christ's own life and death.

Dealing with End-of-Life Issues

Most Americans say they would like to die at home, but the reality is that 80 percent of them will die in some kind of healthcare facility. It is comforting to think you will be surrounded by family; the reality is you will probably be surrounded by hospital machines. It is nice to think death will be a humane transition, but the reality is most people will have an institutionalized death in a medical care facility. You can think about dying, prepare for it, and plan for it. The odds it will happen as you planned are very slim.

Retirement is about quality of life, but it is also about recognizing our mortality and planning for the quality of our death. We do not want to be morbid about our approach to death, nor do we want to talk about death too much or too soon. Neither should we ignore it or treat it as something one just does not speak about. For people of faith, life is all about searching for a permanent home, and so dealing with dying is something for a couple to do together and for a family to discuss together. There are so many important decisions on which everyone needs clear understanding of a person's intentions that this is a topic that we should discuss in advance. It is strange that the one thing all human beings have in common is that they will die, yet it is an issue about which we often feel unprepared. Nowadays, there are organizations that provide medical, emotional, or spiritual support to the dying and their families. These organizations focus on the patient's quality of life, dignity, and well-being in the time that remains.

Violent death is not normal, but death is a normal process, and when it runs its course, it can be the person's final act of self-expression. Once a physician has concluded that a particular illness is final and that no cure is likely, the patient enters this final stage of life. Each individual will need to decide whether to fight the diagnosis, try to prove the doctor wrong, and use all that medicine can offer, or whether to adjust to this final stage and simply get the best out of it. The latter patient can still hope for a cure and still take medicine, but the focus turns to what is called palliative care—the comprehensive care, generally of a team, that stresses comfort, relief of pain, physical therapy, emotional support, and spiritual guidance. Hospice is such a team approach, and there are others in hospitals, long-term facilities, and homes and institutions that specialize in the care of the chronically ill.

One of the significant components of dying is pain—physical, emotional, spiritual, and existential.

Christianity encourages the sick to offer up their pain in union with the suffering Christ on the cross and offer it as he did for the salvation of the world. These religious gestures may be ennobling for some, but not for others. It is not necessarily weakness: we need to manage pain as best we can for our own sakes, yes, but also for the sake of our loved ones and our caregivers. The first response of a patient, including Christians and adherents to any other religion, is to remove the pain if that is possible. The second should be to manage the pain with therapies, counseling, education, and medicines both old and new. The third should be to try to transform the pain into a yearning for the afterlife. Finally, if all else fails, and it eventually will, then patients need to tolerate the pain without letting it diminish them with anger, bitterness, resentment, and faithlessness.

Along with planning for death; maintaining quality of life during the dying process; focusing on life's essentials of forgiveness, love, and gratitude; establishing comprehensive care; and managing the pain of final times—we must also stress the importance of finding peace. A dying person must find reconciliation with oneself, with loved ones and friends, with enemies and those who have betrayed them, with their own death, and with God. One must seek reconciliation, peace, acceptance, and surrender to the life one has lived and to the death one must face. This is the time for meditation, reflection, music, serious discussion with a mentor or friend, and prayer. Spiritual reading, scriptures, and poetry can stimulate the needed reflection. Part of the process of finding peace is coping with grief. Those left behind will grieve our loss in death, but the one who is dying grieves now—their former health, a life messed up, opportunities missed, blessings ignored, love unreciprocated, the loss of loved ones and this world, and so on.

Anticipating death can be, above all, a celebration of life. A dying person is going to be missed by loved ones. So, dying can also be a time to celebrate, to tell stories, to share values, and to joyfully share the highlights of one's life. I know several individuals who have written ethical wills to pass on their values, made videos of their last statements to their families, written their own life stories for family members to read, made quilts that became a visual history of important events in their life, or just simply told stories that passed on values.

Things you can do to prepare for dying

- Visit a hospital.
- Interview someone in a hospice.
- Speak to a funeral director.
- Ask friends to talk about when they helped someone make preparations for their death.
- Talk to someone who has lost a spouse in death.
- Meet with your pastor to discuss afterlife.
- Read a book on death and dying.

- Check Web sites on aging and dying, hospice, and so on.
- Initiate a first discussion with family members about your own death.

Dying is an important transition, a time for celebration, and a time for grief. We should not clutter up such an important time with distracting problems or unresolved issues of a practical financial nature that could lead to disagreements among family members. Sorting out our finances can guarantee a smooth transition after death. This final arrangement of finances, done in advance, can be a nice gesture of practical love to those who remain.

Indicating Your Wishes before Death

One of the important rights of all retired people as they approach their final transition into death is to make sure they have as much control as possible over all components of this final phase. As long as you can make decisions, you can control your own finances and accept or refuse treatments and medications. However, what will happen when you become so ill that you cannot understand what the doctor tells you? When you cannot appreciate the consequences of the treatment or its absence? When you cannot sort out the pros and cons of financial decisions? Or when you lose the ability to make these decisions?

Death is, above all, the culminating experience of faith, but if you are incapacitated, who will make sure that your death is the experience of faith that you wanted it to be? It is important to plan ahead and to make sure that there is someone who understands and loves you, who appreciates your values, who will respect your wishes, and who will make sure other people do too. You must designate this person or these persons in advance. If you do not make provisions, some states can initiate legal action and appoint a guardian for you. Moreover, if you do not make important decisions in advance, then you may be left to struggle with these issues in the acute, chronic, and terminal phases of an illness.

Some important decisions that may arise when you are no longer capable of making them

- Decisions on financial matters, such as where to find the money needed to pay healthcare or long-term care services

- Decisions on closing down and selling your home when it is clear you will never return

- Distribution of trust funds you may have established or be involved in

- The kind of care you want when you become incapacitated

- Available treatments to keep you alive as long as possible
- Medical procedures you do or do not want to receive
- Organ donation
- Refusal of exceptional means to prolong your life

To take care of the above decisions and others like them, you can grant someone you trust a durable power of attorney or a durable power of attorney for healthcare issues. You can create a living will that details your wishes and how they are to be carried out. You can carry an organ donor card to notify others which organs you wish to donate. One way or another you must make your wishes clear—ahead of time. Here are common ones.

When I die, I would like the following:

1. I would like to be at home.

2. I would like to be in the company of my family.

3. I would like the assistance of a religious or spiritual figure.

4. I would like to have all my finances in order.

5. I would like to have clear advance directives available to guide my loved ones.

6. I would like myself and loved ones to have the benefit of hospice care.

It is increasingly common for retirees, in anticipation of their death, to leave, along with their will regarding their estate, a will regarding their values as well. Besides bequeathing your possessions, you can bequeath your values in an ethical will. Such a presentation can be a video or a written statement of one's beliefs, experiences that have enlightened a person, lessons one has learned, hopes and dreams for spouse, family, and friends. There are now books and experts who can help you in writing your ethical will (www.ethicalwill.com). This is a wonderful way of drawing together a lot of what is happening in the process of dying, as one looks back over life, evaluates one's achievements and failures, and longs to see loved ones flourish. Ethical wills represent ways in which a person getting ready for death endeavors to make their values live on. An ethical will is not a sermon; it is a synthesis of one's life; what one has done, what one is proud of, and what one did not do but hopes their children will do. In general, an ethical will includes spiritual convictions, lessons learned, and people who have been influential.

The Commission on Aging with Dignity has developed an integrated approach to end-of-life decisions, which they call *Five Wishes* (www.agingwithdignity.org). These five decisions are as follows:

1. The person I want to make care decisions for me when I can't

2. The kind of medical treatment I want or don't want

3. How comfortable I want to be

4. How I want people to treat me

5. What I want my loved ones to know

Five Wishes meets all legal requirements in forty states, and it supersedes all previous documents including durable power of attorney, living will, and so on. It is an easy and convenient way of dealing with major issues altogether. It is very clear, very specific. It must be witnessed and/or notarized, depending on the requirements of specific states.

Dying with Dignity

We have considered that dying is an expression of our life. If you learned how to live, dying will come naturally. There will always be pain, loss, grief, anxiety at the unknown, and fear for what lies ahead or for what does not lie ahead. It is important to die well and to take dying seriously. Those who trivialize death by hiding from it or ignoring it make life trivial too. For retirement to be successful, a person must find meaning in his or her life. For retirement to conclude well, a person must find meaning in his or her death. There comes a time when the best years are no longer ahead. Components of a good death would include accepting one's life as it has been, being peaceful with God and with others, letting go contentedly, and drawing to closure with hope.

Death can come unexpectedly at any time, but when it is part of a gradual process, the final stage begins when a doctor gives a patient a terminal diagnosis. This news changes everything. Up until this point, a retiree's focus is wellness and living fully, no matter their condition. With the doctor's communication that an illness is terminal, the focus changes to preparation for death. Of course, for some people with a terminal diagnosis, death can be years away, but once it is terminal a prudent person needs to set in motion the final decisions and responses of life. One already knows with the diagnosis that he or she can gradually or rapidly lose bodily control, mobility control, emotional control, and mental control.

These losses are not inevitable; some people can maintain most of their own functions right to the end. Nevertheless, with a terminal diagnosis one needs to face final issues, make the decisions already described in this chapter, and emphasize one's own focus to loved ones how to deal with the end experiences of life. *Five Wishes* or some clearly articulated desire for a hospice program can give a sense of direction to one's decisions. Still, dying with dignity includes four areas of additional attention:

1. Being comfortable

2. Maintaining personal care

3. Appreciating a sense of community

4. Enjoying religious and spiritual support

As a disease progresses or simply as old age and a loss of interest in living set in, it will become increasingly significant to have established with loved ones and caregivers the kind of comfort levels you would like them to maintain for you. Many visitors—whether family, friends, or even acquaintances—would love to do something to make you more comfortable, but often just do not know what you would like. You can always draw up a list of your wishes for maintaining adequate comfort levels:

1. I would like medication to relieve pain whenever the doctor allows it.

2. I do not want an attending physician who imposes his or her nonmedical, religious, or philosophical views on me as a patient.

3. I want to be maintained in good mental and emotional health as long as possible through medication and counseling. I do not want to be left to drift into depression.

4. I want those who attend me to keep in mind simple things that can facilitate comfort—moist cloths on face, lips, hands, neck; warm baths as often as possible; massages of joints and back.

5. I would like to listen to my favorite music frequently; my child/children know what it is.

We hear horror stories of the elderly being abused in long-term care facilities. Let us hope our family will make sure this does not happen. However, we must go beyond the avoidance of abuse to the daily maintenance of personal care. Again, let people know what you want:

1. I wish to have my physical appearance reflect the care I have always shown. Please make sure someone shaves me, cuts my nails, cleans my teeth and rinses my mouth, and keeps my hair cut and tidy.

2. I must be kept clean at all times. I do not want anyone coming into my room and thinking I am unclean, or that I have an offensive odor.

3. The clothes I wear must be clean and tidy and changed frequently. If I need new ones, please buy them.

Relationships are always important, and many retirees have had added opportunity to foster relationships of family, old and new friends, possibly discussion or church groups. Individuals who have appreciated a sense of community do not suddenly become loners as they become incapable of the kind of communication they formerly had. You might remind family and friends of your desire to maintain a sense of community even as you move closer to death:

1. I wish to have friends visit me.

2. I want people to talk to me intelligently, even if I cannot reply. I do not want people to talk down to me as I get older.

3. I want to see my child/children and grandchildren and hear their stories.

4. I would like to have photos of loved ones around my room.

5. I would like my loved ones to give me physical contact, hold my hands.

6. As my death approaches, I hope someone will stay with me.

7. I hope the staff will be pleasant and cheerful and treat me as a human being.

I have suggested that questions of life and death, afterlife, God, and eternity become more important as one approaches death. In general, retired people are not more religious or more spiritual than other age groups, nor are they more religious than they were when they were younger. Retirees nearing death do ask about ultimate realities and can benefit from religious and spiritual support. Some elderly who have participated in religion all their lives will find it important in death. Others, too, may find the questioning and discussion helpful. You might want to point this out to your caregivers:

1. I would like members of my faith to be with me from time to time.

2. I wish my pastor, mentor, spiritual guide to visit me.

3. I want someone to read my favorite religious, spiritual, or poetry book(s) to me.

4. If there are religious functions in the healthcare facility where I am, I would like to attend.

5. I would like visitors to pray with me.

Retirement consists of several phases but inevitably includes facing the aging process and the final transition in death. These are the times when our values and faith come to the fore to comfort and strengthen us in this final stage of our journey through life. It will rarely be as we hoped or planned, but we can accept the circumstances with peace. We are not journeying in darkness to the unknown, but being drawn forward by a loving God.

QUESTIONS FOR PERSONAL REFLECTION

1. How has your health deteriorated and how have you coped?

2. What are the major stresses you experience as you get older and how can you manage them?

3. What do you believe awaits you at death?

4. How would you like people to remember you when you die? Have you given them plenty of reasons to remember you in the way you want?

5. What values do you leave to those who follow you?

THINGS TO DO

- Make preventive care a priority.

- Plan ahead individually and with family for a careful management of future needs.

- Set up a living will.

- Plan for the quality of your death.

THINGS TO AVOID

- Letting stress become *distress*

- Being passive when business, healthcare, and political communities ignore the elderly

- Being unprepared for end-of-life issues

- Allowing situations where you have no one appointed to make decisions for you when you cannot

THINGS TO THINK ABOUT

- How sources of stress in your life can be reduced

- How various professionals can help maintain wellness and manage pain

- How you would like to die with dignity

- How you want to be treated at the end

Appendix

I Am a Retiree—and Enjoying It

I am retired!
I've found it hard to accept, Lord.
I guess I did not understand what it means to
  be a retiree.

I always thought of it happening to someone
  else.
Now it has occurred to me
    that I have entered a new stage in my life.
Help me, O Lord, to understand better
    what has happened to me.
What new obligations have I assumed?
How should I deal with the new situations
    in which I find myself?

I have been used to thinking of retirement
    as a time of declining powers.
But now it has dawned upon me that it
    also brings new opportunities and new
    influence.
I thank you, Lord, for bringing me to this new
  stage in life.

Lord, help me use my past experiences well:
  To learn from my mistakes and seek for-
  giveness,
  To turn from selfish concerns to generous
  self-gift,
  To bring healing to myself and others.

The more I look at my retirement years,
The more I see them as a new vocation:
  To be who I want to be,
  To share the riches of my experience,
  To cherish and share your love.

People tell me retirement could be a third of
  my life.
  May it be a time for joyful rest,
  peaceful acceptance,
  and exciting challenges;
A time to rediscover my purpose in life,
  to rekindle love of family and friends,
  to rest peacefully in your presence.

Retirement—a transition, a call, a gift,
  and most of all,
  a time to enjoy life to its fullest.

Further Reading

Robert J. Wicks. *After 50: Spiritually Embracing Your Own Wisdom Years.* New York/Mahwah, NJ: Paulist Press, 1997. This excellent book gives insightful, practical guidance on prayer, community, service, care of others, and personal growth in retirement years.

Richard P. Johnson. *Creating a Successful Retirement: Finding Peace and Purpose.* Liguori, MI: Liguori Publications, 1999. As the title indicates, this very fine book focuses more on psychology than spirituality. It is a perceptive reflection and offers both vision and practical help.

Ernst and Young's Retirement Planning Guide. New York, 2001. Among today's innumerable financial planning guides, this is one of the best and is not afraid to deal with personal and transitional issues.

Ralph Warner. *Get a Life: You Don't Need a Million to Retire Well.* Berkeley, CA: Nolo Books, 1996, 2002, Fourth Edition. Although one of the earlier books on this topic, this is still one of my favorites. The *San Diego Union-Tribune* called this book "A cheerful antidote to the retirement industry's chilling predictions." It is entertaining reading, especially in the earlier chapters, and most particularly chapter 1.

Gail Liberman and Alan Lavine. *Rags to Retirement.* New York: Alpha-Penguin, 2003. This offers twelve stories from people who retired well on much less than one would think. It is a very quick read. They are stories of real people.

Robert K. Otterbourg. *Retire and Thrive.* Washington, DC: Kiplinger Books, 2003. This is interesting reading. The book is also interestingly set out: a combination of reflection, stories of remarkable people who share their retirement strategies, helpful boxes, and quotes. Lots of stories of how remarkable retirees managed their retirement, adapted, worked part-time, and became creative.

Patricia Schultz. *1000 Places to See Before You Die: A Traveler's Life List.* New York: Workman Publishing, 2003. Lots of great ideas and suggestions.

Ernie J. Zelinski. *How to Retire Happy, Wild, and Free.* Berkeley, CA: Ten Speed Press, 2004. This is a great book. It is written very well and is enjoyable to read. It deals with similar topics to those dealt with in the books mentioned above, but deals with them in a lighthearted and easy read.

Abigail Trafford. *My Time: Making the Most of the Rest of Your Life.* New York: Basic Books, 2004. This book deals with the main issues of retirement in an interesting, uncluttered, storytelling style. It is very good.

David Yount. *A Baby Boomer's Guide to Spirituality.* Minneapolis: Fortress Press, 2005. The author urges readers to expand their spirit in retirement, invest in others, and cultivate community. It is a simple, inspirational book that is well written and focused in the right areas for retirees.

Mark Victor Hansen and Art Linkletter. *How to Make the Rest of Your Life the Best of Your Life*. Nashville: Thomas Nelson Books, 2006. An entertaining and lighthearted read.

Connie Goldman and Richard Mahler. *Secrets of Becoming a Late Bloomer*. Minneapolis: Fairview Press, 2007. This recently published book is very good, but it is not really focused on spirituality. It deals with people over 50 and the new opportunities they encounter.